FAMILY FREEZER *Meals*

80+ SLOW COOKER FREEZER RECIPES FOR THE BUSY FAMILY

Family Freezer Meals

To contact the publisher, visit www.OneIdeaPress.com

ISBN-13: 978-1-944134-13-6

Printed in the United States of America

80+ SLOW COOKER FREEZER RECIPES FOR THE BUSY FAMILY

FAMILY FREEZER MEALS

KELLY McNELIS

This book is dedicated to the readers of **THE FAMILY FREEZER** blog. Thank you for trying my recipes and encouraging me to create more of them.

TABLE OF *Contents*

WELCOME

Freezer cooking is about more than just food to me. It's a way to save time so I can devote myself to my family, friends, and hobbies (like reading and running). This became especially important to me when I became a mom in 2009. Time was of the essence as I juggled work, a new baby, and trying to eat healthy. I realized making food ahead of time and freezing it meant I could enjoy birthday parties and holiday gatherings with my family instead of spending the day in the kitchen.

When I was pregnant with my second daughter, I decided I needed to take my freezer cooking to the next level and start prepping meals for everyday life. I wanted to stock my freezer with healthy meals to eat after her birth, and when I went back to work, I wanted to have plenty of meals ready for busy weeknights. This is when I fell in love with slow cooker freezer meals in particular because they didn't require cooking before freezing and were easy to assemble and freeze.

Around the same time, I started a blog, and the response to my slow cooker freezer recipes was overwhelming. It turned out I wasn't alone. Thousands of other people – maybe even millions – were as excited about saving time and eating healthy as me.

Fast forward six years, three more children, thousands of slow cooker recipes, and tons of hard work. The Family Freezer blog is now a full-time business for my husband and me. We make our own hours, pursue work that we enjoy, and spend a lot of time with our family. Sure, slow cooker freezer meals are our business now, but they're also how we manage to feed our family healthy, homemade meals night after night.

This cookbook includes all of my best recipes and tips that I learned over the years of using my slow cooker. You'll find recipes for everyone, including meat-lovers, vegetarians, and people on special diets.

A free printable version of my 10 favorite recipes and a full shopping list is available at thefamilyfreezer.com/freebie.

XOXO,

Kelly

THE BENEFITS OF FREEZER COOKING

• • • • • • • • • • • •

Once you get the hang of freezer cooking, I know you'll be hooked. I simply can't say enough good things about it. The way I see it, there are four major benefits:

SAVE *Time*

All of my recipes are frozen without any cooking ahead of time and cooked later. That means they're very quick and easy to prep, and taste exactly like freshly prepared meals (no "leftover" taste!). You need to set aside time to prep them for the freezer, but most meals only take 5-15 minutes to make, and you only have to clean up your kitchen once, so they save a lot of time in the long run. I like to set aside an hour on the weekend to make 6-8 meals at a time. The day of cooking, you only need to pour the freezer bag into the slow cooker and dinner is done.

SAVE *Money*

Not only will you save time making freezer meals, but you'll save money, too. By keeping your freezer stocked, you'll never have to rely on take-out and other expensive convenience meals. You'll learn how to take advantage of sales and bulk food discounts at the grocery store and turn them into freezer meals. Once you get the hang of making freezer meals, you can even get creative with meat and produce that are going to expire (what a waste of money!) and turn them into freezer meals instead.

EAT *Healthy*

Making freezer meals is an easy way to eat healthy. The USDA Food Safety and Inspection Service says that freezing doesn't break down nutrients, so they're just as nutritious as freshly prepared meals. By preparing your own freezer meals, you'll have total control over which ingredients you use and where you buy them from. You can also make modifications to fit special diets. Full nutritional information is provided for every single recipe in this cookbook so you can decide what is best for your family to eat.

HELP *Others*

Slow cooker freezer meals make great gifts and are an easy way to give someone a home-cooked meal. I make freezer meals for my parents, grandparents, neighbors, pregnant friends, and pretty much everyone else who I know. Other people have told me that they've shared freezer meals with traveling spouses, children in college, friends having surgery, and more. It seems like everyone appreciates a healthy, homemade meal, and making a slow cooker freezer meal doesn't require much time or money on your part. It's a win-win for everyone.

"My favorite thing about freezer meals is that it becomes our family's fast food and thus saves us money when we don't plan so well or the unexpected comes up."

-Cheryl, Facebook fan of **THE FAMILY FREEZER**

GETTING STARTED

• • • • • • • • • • • •

CLEAN OUT YOUR FREEZER

Before you do anything else, do yourself a favor and clean out your freezer to make room for your freezer meals. Make a list of everything that is in your freezer and then brainstorm how you can turn it into meals over the coming week or two. (Think of how much money you'll save!) If anything in your freezer is expired, throw it out (or put it down your garbage disposal). If there is food in your freezer that has been in there for over a year, get rid of it. Does that thought make you feel guilty or wasteful? Let me give you permission to do it anyway. I hate wasting food, but sometimes it needs to be done. You are never going to eat that food and it is holding you back from filling your freezer with healthy slow cooker freezer meals.

When you start stocking your freezer with new slow cooker freezer meals, I recommend using a freezer inventory sheet or even a simple notebook to keep track of everything you make and when it's going to expire. (Most freezer meals last at least three months in a regular freezer.) This will help you with meal planning and you'll never have to waste food again.

INGREDIENTS

The quality of ingredients will affect the taste and nutritional value of your freezer meals. I recommend buying the best ingredients that you can afford and not stressing over the rest. If you can use local, USDA-certified organic vegetables, meats, and dairy products, great. If you can't, or simply don't want to, that's fine, too. If you're trying to decide which foods are most important to buy organic, the Environmental Working Group provides information on which popular produce items have the most pesticide residue. More than anything, I want you to know that you're saving money and eating healthier by making your own meals than eating out.

The quality of meat is especially important in slow cooker freezer meals. I recommend following my ingredient lists exactly, especially if you're new to slow cooker freezer meals or cooking in general. For example, do not replace chicken breasts with tenders or thin-sliced breasts – both of these cuts of meat are more likely to dry out in slow cookers. The cuts of meat included in my recipes have been tested over and over again by my family and the readers of my New Leaf Wellness blog, so I know that they'll turn out great the very first time that you make them. I want every meal that you make to be a huge success.

"My favorite thing about freezer meals is that they make it possible for me to always have a home-cooked, real food, healthy meal no matter how busy my day is, especially when it's a long day that leaves me too tired to cook."

-Heather, Facebook fan of **THE FAMILY FREEZER**

REQUIRED MATERIALS

You don't need fancy equipment to prep slow cooker freezer meals. Heck, you don't even need a kitchen! All you need is a knife, cutting board, and place to work. These meals are so easy to make, friends. You got this.

Here are some of the items that I use when I'm making a bunch of slow cooker meals at once:

- **Gallon-sized plastic freezer bags.** I store my meals in bags because they don't take up a lot of space in the freezer. I like name brand bags, like Hefty and Ziplock. I think they have the best quality and are least likely to leak while freezing or thawing.
- **A Sharpie marker.** I think these are the best markers to use to label freezer bags because they don't wipe off or smear.
- **Freezer meal labels.** If you want to include more information on the

freezer bag (like a list of ingredients or cooking instructions), I recommend adding a label of some kind. You can keep it simple and tape recipe cards to the bags with clear shipping tape or use Avery water-resistant sticker labels. (I buy label number 22827. Each label measures 3.5" x 4.75.")

- **A food chopper.** This is totally optional, but I own a Vidalia Chop Wizard and I love using it to chop onions.
- **Jokari Hands-Free Baggy Clips.** I use these baggy holders to keep my freezer bags upright while I'm filling them. They help me work in an assembly line and keep the bags from spilling food on the floor.
- **An extra freezer.** Most meals will last at least three months in the freezer, but if you want them to last longer, or if you need more space, I recommend purchasing a chest freezer. I own a Kenmore upright freezer. (It is model number 22442 and has 13.8 cubic feet of interior storage capacity.)
- **A slow cooker.** I've tested 5-10 different slow cookers and any one that holds 4-7 quarts will work with my recipes. I use the Crock-Pot Cook & Carry 6-Quart Slow Cooker most often because it has a programmable timer (more info below).

WHAT IS THE BEST SLOW COOKER?

If you've never used a slow cooker before, there are five basic components:

1. Base – the bottom piece of the slow cooker that sits on your countertop.

2. Crock – the bowl that holds the food while cooking.

3. Lid – the piece that sits on top of the crock and holds the heat inside. Some slow cookers have locks that hold the lid in place. (Locks are especially helpful if you cook the food at home and then take it to someone else's house – no mess in the car!)

4. Cooking Temperature – the amount of heat that determines how quickly the food will

TIP

• • • • • • •

Buy frozen diced onions when you're prepping a bunch of freezer meals at once, and substitute one cup of diced onion for each onion in the recipe. This will save you so much time and tears!

cook. Most slow cookers have three settings: low (for longer cooking times), high (for quicker cooking times), and warm (to keep cooked food warm until it's time to eat it). I cook all of my meals on the low setting, but you can switch to high and cut the cooking time in half.

5. Timer – the ability to program how long the food will cook. You enter an amount of time that you want the food to cook (for example, 8 hours) and the slow cooker automatically switches to the "warm" setting after that. This feature is not available on all slow cookers.

Most slow cookers contain the same components; the biggest differences are the size of the crock and whether or not it has a timer.

All of my recipes are written for 4-7-quart slow cookers and typically have 4-6 servings. If you are cooking for two or more people, I recommend buying a slow cooker in this size range and making the recipes as written. They're designed to use ingredients in their entirety (for example, a whole can of beans and a pound of meat), and any leftovers from the meal can be eaten for lunch or dinner the next day or frozen for later.

If you are only cooking for one person or absolutely hate leftovers, I recommend cutting the recipes in half and purchasing a smaller slow cooker (2-4 quarts). A smaller slow cooker will ensure that your meal doesn't overcook or burn. If you still want to use all of the ingredients, you can split each recipe into two freezer bags. Keep the cooking times the same.

Whether or not you purchase a slow cooker with a timer is up to you, but I highly recommend one. Timers help make sure meals with shorter cooking times (like recipes with chicken breasts) aren't overcooked, and they're very helpful if you work full-time and are out of the house for more than eight hours a day.

I'm currently using the Crock-Pot Cook & Carry 6-Quart Slow Cooker most often, but I'm constantly testing new models, so if you want to know which one I'm using, send me an email or find me on social media. I'd be happy to help you figure out which model is best for you.

THE **BEST** AND **WORST** FOODS TO FREEZE

All of the recipes in this cookbook freeze well, but I'd like to give you some guidance on what freezes well (and what doesn't) so you can decide if you want to turn some of your family-favorite recipes into slow cooker freezer meals.

Best

- Anything that can be cooked in the slow cooker without any cooking ahead of time.
- Meat – beef, chicken, pork, etc.
- One-pot meals that are often cooked in big pots on the stovetop, like chili, stew, and soup (especially if they're not creamy or milk-based).

TIP

Sweet potatoes tend to freeze better than white potatoes.

Worst

- Some meals with dairy products (like mayonnaise, cream cheese, and sour cream). I usually wait to add dairy until the last 15-30 minutes of cooking so it doesn't curdle.
- Raw potatoes. It's possible to include raw potatoes in your slow cooker freezer meals, but they're tricky. I recommend using the freshest potatoes that you can find, waiting until the last minute to cut them, and freezing them quickly after that.
- Fruits and vegetables with a high water content, like melons and lettuce.
- Fresh broccoli tends to oxidize quickly if it isn't cooked before freezing. That means it can turn brown and not taste very good after being frozen raw. Why does this happen with broccoli and not other fresh vegetables? I don't know, but I always use store-bought frozen broccoli in my freezer recipes instead of fresh.

ASSEMBLING SLOW COOKER FREEZER MEALS

Slow cooker freezer meals don't require any cooking before freezing, so they're very quick and easy to make. But wait – is it really safe to freeze raw meat with vegetables? Yes! Let me assure you that it's perfectly safe. The USDA Food Safety and Inspection Service explains that the freezer inactivates any microbes present in food (like bacteria, yeasts, and molds). Plus, don't forget that you'll cook the meals before eating them, just like you do every other day with meat and vegetables.

I like to set aside an hour or two on the weekend to make 6-10 slow cooker freezer meals at a time. Here's what my process looks like:

1. I print my recipes and shopping list ahead of time and go grocery shopping. This saves me time on prep day, and gives me more energy to make the meals. If you're going to make a lot of meals, just make sure there is enough room in your refrigerator and freezer for all of the ingredients.

2. I try to set aside a chunk of time to make the meals when I won't be interrupted. This means planning ahead so my husband can be in charge of our five children.

3. When I'm making the meals, I typically fill the freezer bags in an assembly line. I like to get all of the peeling and chopping of fresh vegetables out of the way and wait to use my cutting board for meat until the very end. (That way, I only have to wash it once.) If you're brand new to freezer meals or feel overwhelmed by the thought of reading multiple recipes at once, just fill one bag at a time before moving onto the next.

4. Probably my most important tip for freezer meal prep day is to play music, have fun, and give yourself a pat on the back when you're done. You'll be much more likely to continue making freezer meals in the future if you enjoy the process.

LABEL YOUR MEALS

It's easiest to label your freezer bags before you fill them. The bags are flat and clean (and don't have any condensation on them). It's tempting to skip this step and jump right into filling the bags, but after a few weeks or months, you probably won't remember what is in each bag and how to cook it if it isn't labeled. Including cooking instructions is especially helpful if someone else will be cooking the meal, like your spouse or a teenager.

Label your slow cooker freezer meals with the following:

- The name of the recipe.
- The ingredients (optional, but nice if you're going to share the meal with someone else who might be on a special diet or have a food allergy).
- The cooking instructions. Make sure to note if the meal needs to be thawed and ingredients, if any, that need to be added the day of cooking (for example, chicken broth).
- The expiration or "use by" date. Most slow cooker freezer meals will last at least three months in a standard freezer attached to a refrigerator.

PACKAGING

If you package and store your freezer meals correctly, you should not have any problems with leaking or freezer burn.

TIP

Since slow cooker meals don't require any cooking before freezing, they technically don't need to be made in a kitchen. If you're prepping freezer meals with a group, feel free to spread to any available surface, like a dining table.

I store all of my slow cooker freezer meals in gallon-sized plastic freezer bags. Bags stack easily in the freezer and don't take up a lot of space. They're also quick and easy to thaw. If you don't like the idea of using disposable bags, you can wash and reuse them after cooking the meals.

I recommend using name brand freezer bags. I have tried cheaper, generic brands, but they tend to tear and leak.

When you're making slow cooker freezer meals, fill your freezer bags in this order:

Veggies and beans at the bottom.

Sauces and spices in the middle (so they don't get left in the freezer bag).

Meat at the top (so it's the first ingredient poured into the slow cooker by the heating source).

Remove as much air as possible before sealing the bag. This is important because it will help your meal stay fresh longer and prevent freezer burn. Not removing enough air is one of the most common mistakes made by freezer cooking newbies! So, what is the best way to remove air from freezer bags?

Here are some suggestions:

Old fashioned elbow grease. I like to pinch the bag right above the ingredients and fold it so that all of the air comes out of the top before closing the seal. Then, I release the fold and pat the bag so the ingredients are evenly distributed.

A vacuum sealer. I own a food saver, but it works best with meals that don't have a lot of liquid. Liquid is only suctioned from the bag, filling up the drip tray, and leaving the bag unable to be sealed. Since most of my freezer meals include sauce, this machine won't work well.

Dip the bag in water. I haven't tried this method myself, but several blog readers told me that can you dip the bottom of the freezer bag in water and seal the bag after the air is forced to the top.

After sealing your freezer bags, distribute the contents of the bag as evenly as possible so your meal can be frozen flat and stacked in your freezer to save space.

THAWING FREEZER MEALS

Most freezer meals need to be thawed before cooking. Thawing helps your meal cook evenly, quickly, and safely (especially for meals with raw meat). It will also help the frozen meal fit in your slow cooker. (Because it's hard to fit a frozen square block in an oval-shaped slow cooker!)

There are three safe ways to thaw slow cooker freezer meals:

- In the refrigerator overnight.
- In the morning in water.
- In the morning in the microwave. (This can be tricky because you'll need to transfer the freezer meal from its plastic bag to a microwave safe dish. .

After thawing, cook immediately.

I know it can be tough to remember to thaw meals ahead of time, so I put together a list of easy ways to remember to move your meal from the freezer to the refrigerator:

1. Set a reminder on your phone. (This is my husband's favorite method.)
2. Associate thawing meals with something that you do every day, like cleaning up your kitchen after dinner.
3. Ask your kids. or spouse to remind you.
4. Plans your meals ahead of time and write them in your planner.

5. Keep a copy of your meal plan everywhere you can possibly see it. (I like to hang a printed calendar on my refrigerator and keep a digital list on my computer and phone in an app.)
6. Stick a Post-it Note to your freezer door.
7. Display your weekly meal plan in your home where you can't help but see it. (This is my favorite method. We have a chalkboard hanging in our dining room that I update weekly with a list of dinners for that week.)
8. Write yourself a note and place it on the kitchen counter.
9. Keep your slow cooker sitting on your kitchen counter.
10. Hang your car keys on a magnetic hook attached to the freezer.

If you forget to thaw your meal in the refrigerator, thaw it in water in the morning. It doesn't have to be 100% thawed - just make sure you can break up the contents of the bag and dump all of them into the slow cooker.

• • • • • • • • • • •

"I love making freezer meals because, to be honest, I am not a very good cook. With freezer meals, I know I can make good, healthy, delicious meals at home."

-Lisa, Facebook fan of **THE FAMILY FREEZER**

• • • • • • • • • • •

Slow Cooker
FREEZER RECIPES

Beef

BEEF, LIME & CILANTRO CHILI

SERVES 6

INGREDIENTS

1 LB 85% LEAN GROUND BEEF

14.5oz CAN TOMATO SAUCE

1 SMALL YELLOW ONION, DICED

2 TEASPOONS GROUND CUMIN

14.5oz CAN PETITE DICED TOMATOES, UNDRAINED

2 CANS BLACK BEANS (15oz EACH), DRAINED AND RINSED

1/4 CUP FRESH CILANTRO (NOT NEEDED UNTIL DAY OF COOKING)

THE JUICE AND ZEST OF 1 LIME

2 CLOVES GARLIC, MINCED

1 TABLESPOON CHILI POWDER

TO FREEZE AND COOK LATER

1. LABEL YOUR FREEZER BAG WITH THE NAME OF THE RECIPE, COOKING INSTRUCTIONS, AND "USE BY" DATE (THREE MONTHS FROM WHEN YOU PREPPED THE MEAL).
2. ADD ALL INGREDIENTS TO YOUR FREEZER BAG, EXCEPT CILANTRO.
3. REMOVE AS MUCH AIR AS POSSIBLE, SEAL, AND FREEZE FOR UP TO THREE MONTHS.

TO COOK AND ENJOY

1. THAW FREEZER MEAL OVERNIGHT IN REFRIGERATOR, OR IN MORNING IN WATER.
2. ADD CONTENTS OF FREEZER BAG TO CROCKPOT.
3. COOK ON "LOW" SETTING FOR 6 HOURS IN 6-QUART CROCKPOT, OR 8-10 HOURS IN 4-QUART CROCKPOT.
4. BREAK APART BEEF AND STIR.
5. TOP WITH CILANTRO.

NUTRITIONAL INFORMATION

SERVING SIZE: 1 2/3 cups
FAT: 6g
SODIUM: 940mg
CARBS: 32g
SUGAR: 5g
PROTEIN: 24g

CHERRY POT ROAST W/ SWEET POTATOES

SERVES 6

INGREDIENTS

2 LB BONELESS BEEF CHUCK ROAST, FAT TRIMMED

1 SMALL YELLOW ONION, CHOPPED

4 CLOVES GARLIC, MINCED

2 MEDIUM SIZED SWEET POTATOES, PEELED AND CUT INTO 1" PIECES

12oz BAG FROZEN PITTED DARK SWEET CHERRIES

3 TABLESPOONS EXTRA VIRGIN OLIVE OIL

1 TEASPOON THYME

1/2 TEASPOON SALT

1/2 TEASPOON PEPPER

TO FREEZE AND COOK LATER

1. LABEL YOUR FREEZER BAG WITH THE NAME OF THE RECIPE, COOKING INSTRUCTIONS, AND "USE BY" DATE (THREE MONTHS FROM WHEN YOU PREPPED THE MEAL).
2. ADD ALL INGREDIENTS TO YOUR FREEZER BAG.
3. REMOVE AS MUCH AIR AS POSSIBLE, SEAL, AND FREEZE FOR UP TO THREE MONTHS.

TO COOK AND ENJOY

1. THAW FREEZER MEAL OVERNIGHT IN REFRIGERATOR, OR IN MORNING IN WATER.
2. ADD CONTENTS OF FREEZER BAG TO CROCKPOT.
3. COOK ON "LOW" SETTING FOR 6 HOURS IN 6-QUART CROCKPOT, OR 8-10 HOURS IN 4-QUART CROCKPOT.

NUTRITIONAL INFORMATION

SERVING SIZE: 1/3 cup
FAT: 12g
SODIUM: 340mg
CARBS: 21g
SUGAR: 11g
PROTEIN: 35g

HOMEMADE MISSISSIPPI ROAST

SERVES 4

INGREDIENTS

2 LB BONELESS BEEF CHUCK ROAST, FAT TRIMMED

4 PEPPERONCINI PEPPERS

2 LBS CARROTS, PEELED & CHOPPED INTO 1" PIECES

AU JUS SEASONING PACKET

(Make your own homemade seasoning packet from the recipe on page 200!)

1 STICK UNSALTED BUTTER

RANCH SEASONING PACKET

(Make your own homemade seasoning packet from the recipe on page 200!)

TO FREEZE AND COOK LATER

1. LABEL YOUR FREEZER BAG WITH THE NAME OF THE RECIPE, COOKING INSTRUCTIONS, AND "USE BY" DATE (THREE MONTHS FROM WHEN YOU PREPPED THE MEAL).
2. ADD ALL INGREDIENTS TO YOUR FREEZER BAG.
3. REMOVE AS MUCH AIR AS POSSIBLE, SEAL, AND FREEZE FOR UP TO THREE MONTHS.

TO COOK AND ENJOY

1. THAW FREEZER MEAL OVERNIGHT IN REFRIGERATOR, OR IN MORNING IN WATER.
2. ADD CONTENTS OF FREEZER BAG TO CROCKPOT.
3. COOK ON "LOW" SETTING FOR 8 HOURS, OR UNTIL BEEF IS TENDER.
4. SHRED BEEF AND SERVE W/ CARROTS IN CROCKPOT.

NUTRITIONAL INFORMATION

SERVING SIZE: 1/2 cup
FAT: 30g
SODIUM: 1260mg
CARBS: 25g
SUGAR: 11g
PROTEIN: 50g

CHILI-SPICED BEEF & CARROTS

SERVES 4

INGREDIENTS

2 LB BONELESS BEEF CHUCK ROAST, FAT TRIMMED

2 TABLESPOONS RED WINE VINEGAR

1 TABLESPOON CHILI POWDER

1/2 TEASPOON SALT

2 LBS CARROTS, PEELED & CHOPPED INTO 1" PIECES

3 TABLESPOONS EXTRA VIRGIN OLIVE OIL

1/2 TEASPOON GROUND CUMIN

1/2 TEASPOON PAPRIKA

1/2 TEASPOON CRUSHED RED PEPPER FLAKES

1/2 TEASPOON GARLIC POWDER

1/2 TEASPOON ONION POWDER

TO FREEZE AND COOK LATER

1. LABEL YOUR FREEZER BAG WITH THE NAME OF THE RECIPE, COOKING INSTRUCTIONS, AND "USE BY" DATE (THREE MONTHS FROM WHEN YOU PREPPED THE MEAL).
2. ADD ALL INGREDIENTS TO YOUR FREEZER BAG.
3. REMOVE AS MUCH AIR AS POSSIBLE, SEAL, AND FREEZE FOR UP TO THREE MONTHS.

TO COOK AND ENJOY

1. THAW FREEZER MEAL OVERNIGHT IN REFRIGERATOR, OR IN MORNING IN WATER.
2. ADD CONTENTS OF FREEZER BAG TO CROCKPOT.
3. COOK ON "LOW" SETTING FOR 8 HOURS, OR UNTIL BEEF IS TENDER.
4. SHRED BEEF AND SERVE.

NUTRITIONAL INFORMATION

SERVING SIZE: 1/2 cup
FAT: 19g
SODIUM: 650mg
CARBS: 23g
SUGAR: 11g
PROTEIN: 53g

CLASSIC POT ROAST

SERVES 6

INGREDIENTS

2 LB BONELESS BEEF CHUCK ROAST, FAT TRIMMED

1 SMALL YELLOW ONION, PEELED & QUARTERED

1/4 CUP DRIED ONION FLAKES

1 LB CARROTS, PEELED & CHOPPED INTO 1" PIECES

1 LB RUSSET POTATOES, WASHED & CUT INTO 1" PIECES

1/4 TEASPOON ONION POWDER

1/4 TEASPOON CELERY SEED

1 CUP FAT-FREE, LOWER-SODIUM BEEF BROTH (NOT NEEDED UNTIL DAY OF COOKING)

1/4 TEASPOON PAPRIKA

1/4 TEASPOON PEPPER

1/4 TEASPOON DRIED PARSLEY

TO FREEZE AND COOK LATER

1. LABEL YOUR FREEZER BAG WITH THE NAME OF THE RECIPE, COOKING INSTRUCTIONS, AND "USE BY" DATE (THREE MONTHS FROM WHEN YOU PREPPED THE MEAL).
2. ADD ALL INGREDIENTS, EXCEPT BEEF BROTH TO YOUR FREEZER BAG.
3. REMOVE AS MUCH AIR AS POSSIBLE, SEAL, AND FREEZE FOR UP TO THREE MONTHS.

TO COOK AND ENJOY

1. THAW FREEZER MEAL OVERNIGHT IN REFRIGERATOR, OR IN MORNING IN WATER.
2. ADD CONTENTS OF FREEZER BAG & BEEF BROTH TO CROCKPOT.
3. COOK ON "LOW" SETTING FOR 8 HOURS, OR UNTIL BEEF IS TENDER.

NUTRITIONAL INFORMATION

SERVING SIZE: 1/3 cup
FAT: 5g
SODIUM: 480mg
CARBS: 25g
SUGAR: 6g
PROTEIN: 38g

GRANDMA'S BEEF STEW

SERVES 5

INGREDIENTS

1 LB BONELESS BEEF CHUCK ROAST, FAT TRIMMED & CUT INTO 1" PIECES

1 SMALL YELLOW ONION, PEELED AND CHOPPED

2 CLOVES GARLIC, MINCED

1 TEASPOON DRIED THYME

2 RUSSET POTATOES, PEELED AND CHOPPED INTO 1" SQUARES

1 LB CARROTS, PEELED & CHOPPED

1 TEASPOON DRIED ROSEMARY

1 BAY LEAF

1/2 TEASPOON SALT

1/4 TEASPOON PEPPER

2 CUPS FAT-FREE, LOWER-SODIUM BEEF BROTH (NOT NEEDED UNTIL DAY OF COOKING)

4 CUPS WATER (NOT NEEDED UNTIL DAY OF COOKING)

TO FREEZE AND COOK LATER

1. LABEL YOUR FREEZER BAG WITH THE NAME OF THE RECIPE, COOKING INSTRUCTIONS, AND "USE BY" DATE (THREE MONTHS FROM WHEN YOU PREPPED THE MEAL).
2. ADD ALL INGREDIENTS, EXCEPT BEEF BROTH & WATER TO YOUR FREEZER BAG.
3. REMOVE AS MUCH AIR AS POSSIBLE, SEAL, AND FREEZE FOR UP TO THREE MONTHS.

TO COOK AND ENJOY

1. THAW FREEZER MEAL OVERNIGHT IN REFRIGERATOR, OR IN MORNING IN WATER.
2. ADD CONTENTS OF FREEZER BAG, BEEF BROTH & WATER TO CROCKPOT.
3. COOK ON "LOW" SETTING FOR 8 HOURS, OR UNTIL BEEF IS TENDER.
4. REMOVE BAY LEAF.

NUTRITIONAL INFORMATION

SERVING SIZE: 2 cups
FAT: 3g
SODIUM: 110mg
CARBS: 35g
SUGAR: 6g
PROTEIN: 29g

ITALIAN-STYLE POT ROAST

SERVES 6

INGREDIENTS

2 LB BONELESS BEEF CHUCK SHOULDER ROAST

1 SMALL YELLOW ONION, DICED

2 CLOVES GARLIC, MINCED

1/4 CUP HONEY

28oz CAN DICED TOMATOES, UNDRAINED

2 TABLESPOONS EXTRA VIRGIN OLIVE OIL

1 TEASPOON DRIED OREGANO

1/2 TEASPOON DRIED PARSLEY

1/2 TEASPOON SALT

1/4 TEASPOON GROUND BLACK PEPPER

1/4 TEASPOON CRUSHED RED PEPPER FLAKES

TO FREEZE AND COOK LATER

1. LABEL YOUR FREEZER BAG WITH THE NAME OF THE RECIPE, COOKING INSTRUCTIONS, AND "USE BY" DATE (THREE MONTHS FROM WHEN YOU PREPPED THE MEAL).
2. ADD ALL INGREDIENTS TO YOUR FREEZER BAG.
3. REMOVE AS MUCH AIR AS POSSIBLE, SEAL, AND FREEZE FOR UP TO THREE MONTHS.

TO COOK AND ENJOY

1. THAW FREEZER MEAL OVERNIGHT IN REFRIGERATOR, OR IN MORNING IN WATER.
2. ADD CONTENTS OF FREEZER BAG TO CROCKPOT.
3. COOK ON "LOW" SETTING FOR 8 HOURS, OR UNTIL BEEF IS TENDER.
4. SHRED BEEF AND SERVE.

NUTRITIONAL INFORMATION

SERVING SIZE: 1/3 cup
FAT: 10g
SODIUM: 600mg
CARBS: 21g
SUGAR: 16g
PROTEIN: 35g

SPICY BEEF CURRY STEW

SERVES 4

INGREDIENTS

1 LB BONELESS BEEF CHUCK SHOULDER ROAST, FAT TRIMMED & CUT INTO BITE-SIZED PIECES

1 SMALL YELLOW ONION, PEELED & CHOPPED

2 CLOVES GARLIC, MINCED

28oz CAN DICED TOMATOES, UNDRAINED

2 RUSSET POTATOES, PEELED & CHOPPED INTO 1 IN SQUARES

1 LBS CARROTS, PEELED & CHOPPED

2 TABLESPOONS CURRY POWDER

1 TEASPOON CRUSHED RED PEPPER FLAKES

1" FRESH GINGER ROOT, PEELED AND MINCED

2 CUPS FAT-FREE, LOWER SODIUM BEEF BROTH (NOT NEEDED UNTIL DAY OF COOKING)

TO FREEZE AND COOK LATER

1. LABEL YOUR FREEZER BAG WITH THE NAME OF THE RECIPE, COOKING INSTRUCTIONS, AND "USE BY" DATE (THREE MONTHS FROM WHEN YOU PREPPED THE MEAL).
2. ADD ALL INGREDIENTS TO YOUR FREEZER BAG.
3. REMOVE AS MUCH AIR AS POSSIBLE, SEAL, AND FREEZE FOR UP TO THREE MONTHS.

TO COOK AND ENJOY

1. THAW FREEZER MEAL OVERNIGHT IN REFRIGERATOR, OR IN MORNING IN WATER.
2. ADD CONTENTS OF FREEZER BAG & BEEF BROTH TO CROCKPOT.
3. COOK ON "LOW" SETTING FOR 8 HOURS, OR UNTIL BEEF IS TENDER.

NUTRITIONAL INFORMATION

SERVING SIZE: 2.5 cups
FAT: 4g
SODIUM: 1500mg
CARBS: 55g
SUGAR: 15g
PROTEIN: 38g

BEEF & QUINOA STUFFED PEPPERS

SERVES 4

INGREDIENTS

PEPPERS

6 SMALL RED BELL PEPPERS, TOPS IN MIX

1/2 CUP DRY QUINOA, UNCOOKED

1 LB 85% LEAN GROUND BEEF

1 SMALL YELLOW ONION, DICED

1 TABLESPOON ITALIAN

SEASONING

4 CLOVES GARLIC, MINCED

1 TEASPOON SALT

1/2 TEASPOON PEPPER

SAUCE

15oz CAN TOMATO SAUCE

1 TABLESPOON ITALIAN SEASONING

TO FREEZE AND COOK LATER

1. LABEL YOUR FREEZER BAG WITH THE NAME OF THE RECIPE, COOKING INSTRUCTIONS, AND "USE BY" DATE (THREE MONTHS FROM WHEN YOU PREPPED THE MEAL).
2. CUT OFF TOPS OF PEPPERS, CLEAN, & SET ASIDE.
3. IN A LARGE BOWL, MIX DICED TOPS OF PEPPERS W/ REMAINING "PEPPERS" INGREDIENTS.
4. SPOON INTO PEPPERS (1 CUP PER PEPPER), & PLACE IN FREEZER BAG.
5. ADD SAUCE INGREDIENTS TO QUART-SIZED FREEZER BAG.
6. REMOVE AS MUCH AIR AS POSSIBLE FROM BOTH BAGS, SEAL, & FREEZE.

TO COOK AND ENJOY

1. THAW FREEZER MEAL OVERNIGHT IN REFRIGERATOR, OR IN MORNING IN WATER.
2. PLACE STUFFED PEPPERS IN CROCKPOT & COVER W/ SAUCE.
3. COOK ON "LOW" SETTING FOR 6 HOURS IN 6-QUART CROCKPOT, OR 8-10 HOURS IN 4-QUART CROCKPOT.

NUTRITIONAL INFORMATION

SERVING SIZE: 1 PEPPER
FAT: 12g

SODIUM: 620mg
CARBS: 25g

SUGAR: 9g
PROTEIN: 17g

CABBAGE ROLLS W/ WILD RICE

SERVES 6

INGREDIENTS

ROLLS

6 LARGE CABBAGE LEAVES

1 LB 85% LEAN GROUND BEEF

1 CUP DRY WILD RICE, UNCOOKED

1 SMALL YELLOW ONION, DICED

1 TABLESPOON ITALIAN SEASONING

SAUCE

28oz CAN DICED TOMATOES, UNDRAINED

15oz CAN TOMATO SAUCE

1 TABLESPOON HONEY

1 TABLESPOON ITALIAN SEASONING

1/2 TEASPOON SALT

1/2 TEASPOON PEPPER

TO FREEZE AND COOK LATER

1. LABEL YOUR FREEZER BAGS WITH THE NAME OF THE RECIPE, COOKING INSTRUCTIONS, AND "USE BY" DATE (THREE MONTHS FROM WHEN YOU PREPPED THE MEAL).
2. IN A LARGE BOWL, MIX INGREDIENTS FOR CABBAGE ROLL FILLING, & SPOON EQUALLY ONTO LEAVES (2/3 CUP PER LEAF).
3. TUCK IN SIDES, ROLL, & PLACE IN FREEZER BAG (SEAM-SIDE DOWN).
4. ADD SAUCE INGREDIENTS TO YOUR SECOND FREEZER BAG.
5. REMOVE AS MUCH AIR AS POSSIBLE FROM BOTH BAGS, SEAL, & FREEZE.

TO COOK AND ENJOY

1. THAW FREEZER MEAL OVERNIGHT IN REFRIGERATOR, OR IN MORNING IN WATER.
2. PLACE CABBAGE ROLLS IN CROCKPOT AND COVER W/ SAUCE.
3. COOK ON "LOW" SETTING FOR 6 HOURS IN 6-QUART CROCKPOT, OR 8-10 HOURS IN 4-QUART CROCKPOT.

NUTRITIONAL INFORMATION

SERVING SIZE: 1 ROLL
FAT: 11g
SODIUM: 900mg
CARBS: 38g
SUGAR: 12g
PROTEIN: 19g

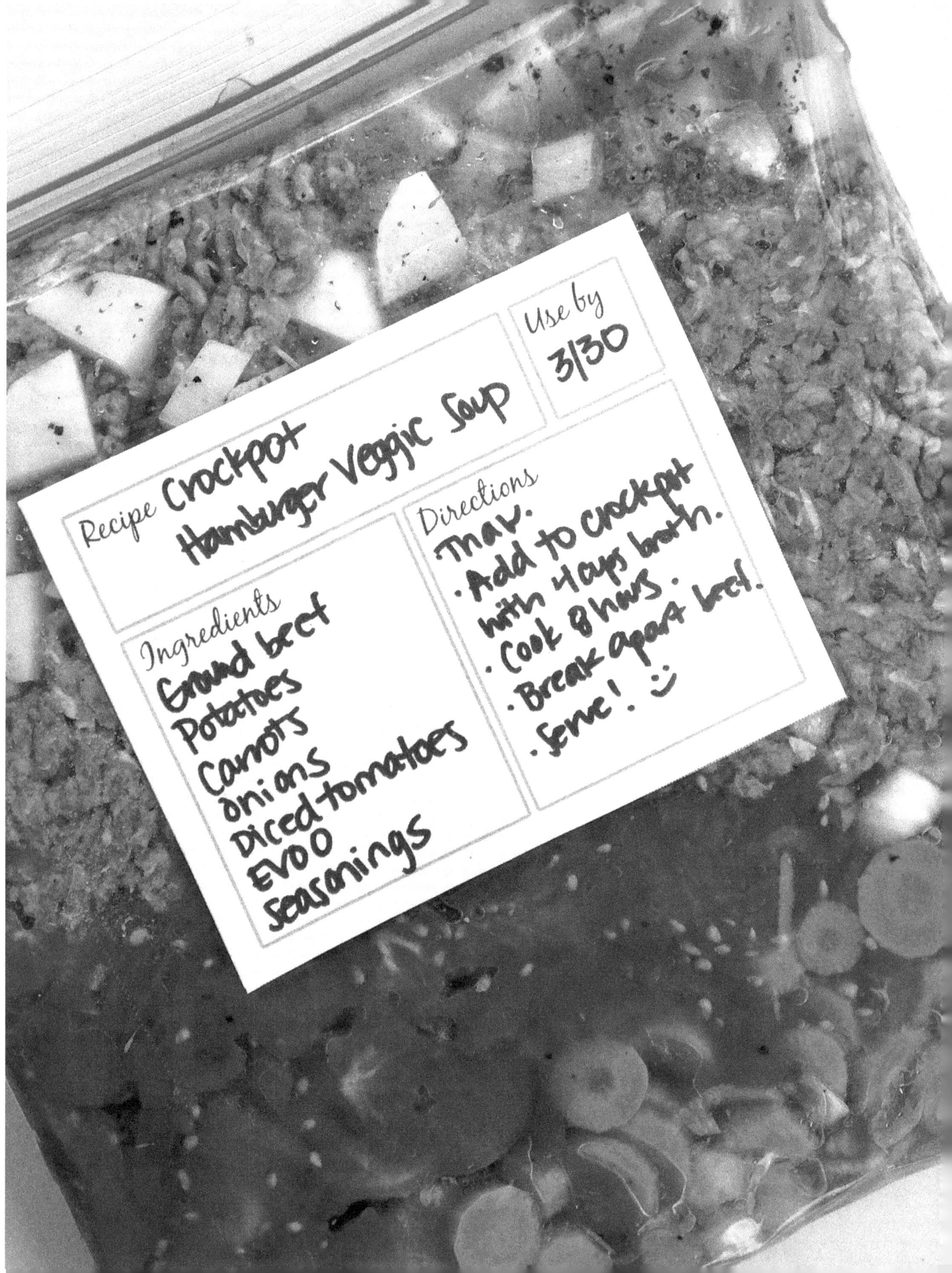

Recipe Crockpot Hamburger Veggie Soup

Use by 3/30

Ingredients
Ground beef
Potatoes
Carrots
Onions
Diced tomatoes
EVOO
Seasonings

Directions
- Thaw.
- Add to crockpot with 4 cups broth.
- Cook 8 hours.
- Break apart beef.
- Serve! :)

HAMBURGER VEGGIE SOUP

SERVES 6

INGREDIENTS

4 LARGE CARROTS, PEELED & SLICED

2 SMALL POTATOES, PEELED AND CUT INTO 1" CHUNKS

1 SMALL ONION, DICED

1 LB 85% LEAN GROUND BEEF

28oz CAN DICED TOMATOES, UNDRAINED

2 CLOVES GARLIC, MINCED

1 TABLESPOON EXTRA VIRGIN OLIVE OIL

1 TABLESPOON ITALIAN SEASONING

1/4 TEASPOON PEPPER

4 CUPS FAT-FREE, LOWER-SODIUM BEEF BROTH (NOT NEEDED UNTIL DAY OF COOKING)

TO FREEZE AND COOK LATER

1. LABEL YOUR FREEZER BAGS WITH THE NAME OF THE RECIPE, COOKING INSTRUCTIONS, AND "USE BY" DATE (THREE MONTHS FROM WHEN YOU PREPPED THE MEAL).
2. ADD ALL INGREDIENTS, EXCEPT BEEF BROTH, TO YOUR FREEZER BAG.
3. REMOVE AS MUCH AIR AS POSSIBLE FROM BOTH BAGS, SEAL, & FREEZE.

TO COOK AND ENJOY

1. THAW FREEZER MEAL OVERNIGHT IN REFRIGERATOR, OR IN MORNING IN WATER.
2. ADD CONTENTS OF FREEZER BAG & BEEF BROTH TO CROCKPOT.
3. COOK ON "LOW" SETTING FOR 8 HOURS, OR UNTIL BEEF IS TENDER.

NUTRITIONAL INFORMATION

SERVING SIZE: 1 2/3 CUP
FAT: 13g
SODIUM: 660mg
CARBS: 19g
SUGAR: 8g
PROTEIN: 18g

ITALIAN MEATBALLS

SERVES 12

INGREDIENTS

MEATBALLS

2 LBS 85% LEAN GROUND BEEF

2 SMALL YELLOW ONIONS, DICED

1/4 CUP DRY QUINOA, UNCOOKED

2 TABLESPOONS APPLE CIDER VINEGAR

1 TABLESPOON ITALIAN SEASONING

2 TEASPOONS GARLIC POWDER

1 TEASPOON WHOLE FENNEL SEED

1 TEASPOON PAPRIKA

1 TEASPOON PEPPER

1/2 TEASPOON RED PEPPER FLAKES

SAUCE

28oz CAN DICED TOMATOES, UNDRAINED

15oz CAN TOMATO SAUCE

1 TABLESPOON HONEY

1 TABLESPOON ITALIAN SEASONING

1/2 TEASPOON SALT

1/2 TEASPOON PEPPER

TO FREEZE AND COOK LATER

1. LABEL YOUR FREEZER BAGS WITH THE NAME OF THE RECIPE, COOKING INSTRUCTIONS, AND "USE BY" DATE (THREE MONTHS FROM WHEN YOU PREPPED THE MEAL).
2. IN A LARGE BOWL, COMBINE MEATBALL INGREDIENTS AND ROLL INTO SMALL BALLS.
3. PLACE IN BAGS.
4. REMOVE AS MUCH AIR AS POSSIBLE FROM BOTH BAGS, SEAL, & FREEZE.

TO COOK AND ENJOY

1. THAW FREEZER MEAL OVERNIGHT IN REFRIGERATOR, OR IN MORNING IN WATER.
2. ADD SAUCE TO CROCKPOT.
3. LAYER MEATBALLS ON TOP OF SAUCE.
4. COOK ON "LOW" SETTING FOR 6 HOURS IN 6-QUART CROCKPOT, OR 8-10 HOURS IN 4-QUART CROCKPOT.

NUTRITIONAL INFORMATION

SERVING SIZE: 3 MEATBALLS
FAT: 11g
SODIUM: 510mg
CARBS: 16g
SUGAR: 8g
PROTEIN: 18g

MINESTRONE SOUP W/ GROUND BEEF

SERVES 6

INGREDIENTS

1 LB 85% LEAN GROUND BEEF

15oz CAN DARK RED KIDNEY BEANS, DRAINED & RINSED

2oz BABY SPINACH (TWO LARGE HANDFULS)

1 SMALL YELLOW ONION, DICED

1 LB BUTTERNUT SQUASH, PEELED & DICED

1 SMALL ZUCCHINI, DICED

14.5oz CAN DICED TOMATOES, UNDRAINED

1 TABLESPOON ITALIAN SEASONING

1 TEASPOON SALT

1 TEASPOON PEPPER

4 CUPS BEEF BROTH (NOT NEEDED UNTIL DAY OF COOKING)

TO FREEZE AND COOK LATER

1. LABEL YOUR FREEZER BAG WITH THE NAME OF THE RECIPE, COOKING INSTRUCTIONS, AND "USE BY" DATE (THREE MONTHS FROM WHEN YOU PREPPED THE MEAL).
2. ADD ALL INGREDIENTS, EXCEPT BEEF BROTH, TO YOUR FREEZER BAG.
3. REMOVE AS MUCH AIR AS POSSIBLE FROM BAG, SEAL, & FREEZE.

TO COOK AND ENJOY

1. THAW FREEZER MEAL OVERNIGHT IN REFRIGERATOR, OR IN MORNING IN WATER.
2. ADD CONTENTS OF FREEZER BAG & BEEF BROTH TO CROCKPOT.
3. COOK ON "LOW" SETTING FOR 6 HOURS IN A 6-QUART CROCKPOT, OR 8-10 HOURS IN A 4-QUART CROCKPOT.
4. BREAK APART BEEF & STIR.

NUTRITIONAL INFORMATION

SERVING SIZE: 1 2/3 CUP
FAT: 11g
SODIUM: 1210mg
CARBS: 29g
SUGAR: 7g
PROTEIN: 21g

STUFFED PEPPER SOUP

SERVES 6

INGREDIENTS

1 LB 85% LEAN GROUND BEEF

1/2 CUP DRY WILD RICE, UNCOOKED

1 GREEN BELL PEPPER, DICED

1 RED BELL PEPPER, DICED

1 SMALL YELLOW ONION, DICED

28oz CAN DICED TOMATOES, UNDRAINED

15oz CAN TOMATO SAUCE

2 CLOVES GARLIC, MINCED

2 TEASPOONS ITALIAN SEASONING

1 TEASPOON SALT

4 CUPS BEEF BROTH (NOT NEEDED UNTIL DAY OF COOKING)

TO FREEZE AND COOK LATER

1. LABEL YOUR FREEZER BAG WITH THE NAME OF THE RECIPE, COOKING INSTRUCTIONS, AND "USE BY" DATE (THREE MONTHS FROM WHEN YOU PREPPED THE MEAL).
2. ADD ALL INGREDIENTS, EXCEPT BEEF BROTH, TO YOUR FREEZER BAG.
3. REMOVE AS MUCH AIR AS POSSIBLE FROM BAG, SEAL, & FREEZE.

TO COOK AND ENJOY

1. THAW FREEZER MEAL OVERNIGHT IN REFRIGERATOR, OR IN MORNING IN WATER.
2. ADD CONTENTS OF FREEZER BAG & BEEF BROTH TO CROCKPOT.
3. COOK ON "LOW" SETTING FOR 6 HOURS IN A 6-QUART CROCKPOT, OR 8-10 HOURS IN A 4-QUART CROCKPOT.
4. BREAK APART BEEF & STIR.

NUTRITIONAL INFORMATION

SERVING SIZE: 2 CUPS
FAT: 12g
SODIUM: 1640mg
CARBS: 26g
SUGAR: 10g
PROTEIN: 19g

CORNED BEEF & CABBAGE

SERVES 8

INGREDIENTS

3 LB BONELESS CORNED BEEF BRISKET

CORNED BEEF SEASONING PACKET

4 RED POTATOES, QUARTERED

3 LB HEAD OF CABBAGE, CORED & ROUGHLY CHOPPED

1/2 LB CARROTS, PEELED & CHOPPED

1/4 CUP APPLE CIDER VINEGAR

1 TABLESPOON DIJON MUSTARD

1/2 CUP HONEY

1/2 TEASPOON CARAWAY SEED

1 TEASPOON PEPPER

TO FREEZE AND COOK LATER

1. LABEL YOUR FREEZER BAG WITH THE NAME OF THE RECIPE, COOKING INSTRUCTIONS, AND "USE BY" DATE (THREE MONTHS FROM WHEN YOU PREPPED THE MEAL).
2. ADD ALL INGREDIENTS TO YOUR FREEZER BAG.
3. REMOVE AS MUCH AIR AS POSSIBLE FROM BAG, SEAL, & FREEZE.

TO COOK AND ENJOY

1. THAW FREEZER MEAL OVERNIGHT IN REFRIGERATOR, OR IN MORNING IN WATER.
2. ADD CONTENTS OF FREEZER BAG TO CROCKPOT.
3. COOK ON "LOW" SETTING FOR 8 HOURS IN A 6-QUART CROCKPOT.

NUTRITIONAL INFORMATION

SERVING SIZE: 1/3 CUP
FAT: 23g
SODIUM: 1470mg
CARBS: 44g
SUGAR: 20g
PROTEIN: 26g

MONSTER CHEESEBURGERS

SERVES 6

INGREDIENTS

2 LBS 85% LEAN GROUND BEEF

1/2 CUP DRIED MINCED ONION

2.5 TEASPOONS MONTREAL STEAK SEASONING

4 SLICES AMERICAN CHEESE (NOT NEEDED UNTIL DAY OF COOKING)

TO FREEZE AND COOK LATER

1. LABEL YOUR FREEZER BAG WITH THE NAME OF THE RECIPE, COOKING INSTRUCTIONS, AND "USE BY" DATE (THREE MONTHS FROM WHEN YOU PREPPED THE MEAL).
2. ADD ALL INGREDIENTS, EXCEPT CHEESE, TO YOUR FREEZER BAG.
3. REMOVE AS MUCH AIR AS POSSIBLE FROM BAG, SEAL, & FREEZE.

TO COOK AND ENJOY

1. THAW FREEZER MEAL OVERNIGHT IN REFRIGERATOR, OR IN MORNING IN WATER.
2. ADD MEAT TO CROCKPOT AND SMOOTH INTO FLAT LAYER OVER THE BOTTOM.
3. COOK ON "LOW" SETTING FOR 6-8 HOURS, OR UNTIL BEEF IS COOKED THROUGH.
4. TOP WITH CHEESE & REPLACE LID FOR 10 MINUTES, OR UNTIL CHEESE IS MELTED.
5. CUT INTO SIX BURGERS & DISCARD GREASE.

NUTRITIONAL INFORMATION

SERVING SIZE: 1 BURGER
FAT: 27g
SODIUM: 680mg
CARBS: 7g
SUGAR: 4g
PROTEIN: 30g

SLOPPY JOES

SERVES 6

INGREDIENTS

1 LB 85% LEAN GROUND BEEF

1 SMALL YELLOW ONION, DICED

1 MEDIUM-SIZED GREEN BELL PEPPER, DICED

15oz CAN TOMATO SAUCE, UNDRAINED

2 TABLESPOONS LIGHT BROWN SUGAR

1 TABLESPOON WORCESTERSHIRE SAUCE

2 TEASPOONS CHILI POWDER

1/2 TEASPOON GARLIC POWDER

1/2 TEASPOON SALT

1/4 TEASPOON PEPPER

1/4 TEASPOON CRUSHED RED PEPPER FLAKES

TO FREEZE AND COOK LATER

1. LABEL YOUR FREEZER BAG WITH THE NAME OF THE RECIPE, COOKING INSTRUCTIONS, AND "USE BY" DATE (THREE MONTHS FROM WHEN YOU PREPPED THE MEAL).
2. ADD ALL INGREDIENTS TO YOUR FREEZER BAG.
3. REMOVE AS MUCH AIR AS POSSIBLE FROM BAG, SEAL, & FREEZE.

TO COOK AND ENJOY

1. THAW FREEZER MEAL OVERNIGHT IN REFRIGERATOR, OR IN MORNING IN WATER.
2. ADD CONTENTS OF FREEZER BAG TO CROCKPOT.
3. COOK ON "LOW" SETTING FOR 6-8 HOURS.
4. CRUMBLE BEEF.
5. STIR.

NUTRITIONAL INFORMATION

SERVING SIZE: 1/2 CUP
FAT: 11g
SODIUM: 670mg
CARBS: 13g
SUGAR: 9g
PROTEIN: 14g

TACO CHILI W/ CORNBREAD TOPPING

SERVES 4

INGREDIENTS

1 LB 85% LEAN GROUND BEEF

1 SMALL YELLOW ONION, DICED

1 GREEN PEPPER, CHOPPED

1 CUP FROZEN CORN

1 TEASPOON HONEY

1/2 TEASPOON SALT

15oz CAN TOMATO SAUCE

1 TABLESPOON CHILI POWDER

1/2 TEASPOON GROUND CUMIN

1/2 TEASPOON CRUSHED RED PEPPER

1/2 TEASPOON PAPRIKA

1/2 TEASPOON GARLIC POWDER

1/2 TEASPOON ONION POWDER

1 CUP SHREDDED CHEDDAR (NOT NEEDED UNTIL DAY OF COOKING)

1 BOX JIFFY CORN MUFFIN MIX & NECESSARY INGREDIENTS ON BOX (NOT NEEDED UNTIL DAY OF COOKING)

TO FREEZE AND COOK LATER

1. LABEL YOUR FREEZER BAG WITH THE NAME OF THE RECIPE, COOKING INSTRUCTIONS, AND "USE BY" DATE (THREE MONTHS FROM WHEN YOU PREPPED THE MEAL).
2. ADD ALL INGREDIENTS, EXCEPT CHEESE AND MUFFIN MIX, TO YOUR FREEZER BAG.
3. REMOVE AS MUCH AIR AS POSSIBLE FROM BAG, SEAL, & FREEZE.

TO COOK AND ENJOY

1. THAW FREEZER MEAL OVERNIGHT IN REFRIGERATOR, OR IN MORNING IN WATER.
2. ADD CONTENTS OF FREEZER BAG TO CROCKPOT.
3. COOK ON "LOW" SETTING FOR 6-8 HOURS.
4. BREAK APART BEEF & TOP CHILI W/ SHREDDED CHEESE AND ASSEMBLED CORNBREAD BATTER.
5. REPLACE LID & COOK FOR ONE HOUR ON "HIGH" SETTING.

NUTRITIONAL INFORMATION

SERVING SIZE: 1/5 SLICE
FAT: 26g
SODIUM: 1310mg
CARBS: 51g
SUGAR: 16g
PROTEIN: 25g

SIMPLE MEATBALL VEGGIE SOUP

SERVES 6

INGREDIENTS

1 LB SMALL MEATBALLS

24oz JAR PASTA SAUCE

1 LB CARROTS, PEELED & CHOPPED

3 CUPS GREEN BEANS, ENDS CUT OFF & CUT INTO BITE-SIZED PIECES

1 LARGE ZUCCHINI, ENDS CUT OFF & CUT INTO BITE-SIZED PIECES

1 SMALL YELLOW ONION, DICED

4 CUPS LOW-SODIUM CHICKEN BROTH (NOT NEEDED UNTIL DAY OF COOKING)

TO FREEZE AND COOK LATER

1. LABEL YOUR FREEZER BAG WITH THE NAME OF THE RECIPE, COOKING INSTRUCTIONS, AND "USE BY" DATE (THREE MONTHS FROM WHEN YOU PREPPED THE MEAL).
2. ADD ALL INGREDIENTS, EXCEPT BROTH, TO YOUR FREEZER BAG.
3. REMOVE AS MUCH AIR AS POSSIBLE FROM BAG, SEAL, & FREEZE.

TO COOK AND ENJOY

1. THAW FREEZER MEAL OVERNIGHT IN REFRIGERATOR, OR IN MORNING IN WATER.
2. ADD CONTENTS OF FREEZER BAG & BROTH TO CROCK-POT.
3. COOK ON "LOW" SETTING FOR 8 HOURS, OR UNTIL CARROTS ARE SOFT.

NUTRITIONAL INFORMATION

SERVING SIZE: 1 2/3 CUP
FAT: 12g
SODIUM: 1000mg
CARBS: 32g
SUGAR: 14g
PROTEIN: 21g

TUSCAN STEAK & GREEN PEPPERS

SERVES 6

INGREDIENTS

2 LB SIRLOIN TIP ROAST, FAT TRIMMED & SLICED

2 GREEN BELL PEPPERS, CHOPPED

4 CLOVES GARLIC, MINCED

14.5oz CAN DICED TOMATOES, UNDRAINED

2 TABLESPOONS EXTRA VIRGIN OLIVE OIL

1 TABLESPOON ITALIAN SEASONING

1 SMALL YELLOW ONION, DICED

1/2 TEASPOON CRUSHED RED PEPPER FLAKES

1 TEASPOON SALT

1/2 TEASPOON PEPPER

TO FREEZE AND COOK LATER

1. LABEL YOUR FREEZER BAG WITH THE NAME OF THE RECIPE, COOKING INSTRUCTIONS, AND "USE BY" DATE (THREE MONTHS FROM WHEN YOU PREPPED THE MEAL).
2. ADD ALL INGREDIENTS TO YOUR FREEZER BAG.
3. REMOVE AS MUCH AIR AS POSSIBLE FROM BAG, SEAL, & FREEZE.

TO COOK AND ENJOY

1. THAW FREEZER MEAL OVERNIGHT IN REFRIGERATOR, OR IN MORNING IN WATER.
2. ADD CONTENTS OF FREEZER BAG TO CROCKPOT.
3. COOK ON "LOW" SETTING FOR 6 HOURS IN A 6-QUART CROCKPOT, OR 8-10 HOURS IN A 4-QUART.

NUTRITIONAL INFORMATION

SERVING SIZE: 1 CUP
FAT: 15g
SODIUM: 630mg
CARBS: 10g
SUGAR: 5g
PROTEIN: 33g

BEEF & SWEET POTATO STEW

SERVES 6

INGREDIENTS

1 1/2 LB STEW MEAT

1 SMALL YELLOW ONION, DICED

4 LARGE CARROTS, PEELED & DICED

1 CUP FROZEN PEAS

2 MEDIUM-SIZED SWEET POTATOES, PEELED & DICED

2 BAY LEAVES

1 TABLESPOON PARSLEY

1 TEASPOON SALT

1 TEASPOON PEPPER

1 TEASPOON GARLIC POWDER

1 TEASPOON ONION POWDER

4 CUPS BEEF BROTH (NOT NEEDED UNTIL DAY OF COOKING)

TO FREEZE AND COOK LATER

1. LABEL YOUR FREEZER BAG WITH THE NAME OF THE RECIPE, COOKING INSTRUCTIONS, AND "USE BY" DATE (THREE MONTHS FROM WHEN YOU PREPPED THE MEAL).
2. ADD ALL INGREDIENTS, EXCEPT BROTH, TO YOUR FREEZER BAG.
3. REMOVE AS MUCH AIR AS POSSIBLE FROM BAG, SEAL, & FREEZE.

TO COOK AND ENJOY

1. THAW FREEZER MEAL OVERNIGHT IN REFRIGERATOR, OR IN MORNING IN WATER.
2. ADD CONTENTS OF FREEZER BAG & BROTH TO CROCKPOT.
3. COOK ON "LOW" SETTING FOR 6 HOURS IN A 6-QUART CROCKPOT, OR 8-10 HOURS IN A 4-QUART.
4. REMOVE BAY LEAVES.
5. BREAK APART BEEF & STIR.

NUTRITIONAL INFORMATION

SERVING SIZE: 1 2/3 CUP
FAT: 5g
SODIUM: 1110mg
CARBS: 19g
SUGAR: 7g
PROTEIN: 28g

Poultry

CHICKEN TIKKA MASALA

INGREDIENTS

2 LBS BONELESS SKINLESS CHICKEN BREAST

2 CLOVES GARLIC, MINCED

2-15oz CANS TOMATO SAUCE

2 TABLESPOONS HONEY

2 TABLESPOONS CURRY POWDER

1/2 TEASPOON ONION POWDER

1/2 TEASPOON SALT

1 TEASPOON CRUSHED RED PEPPER FLAKES

1 CUP HEAVY CREAM

TO FREEZE AND COOK LATER

1. LABEL YOUR FREEZER BAG WITH THE NAME OF THE RECIPE, COOKING INSTRUCTIONS, AND "USE BY" DATE (THREE MONTHS FROM WHEN YOU PREPPED THE MEAL).
2. ADD ALL INGREDIENTS TO YOUR FREEZER BAG.
3. REMOVE AS MUCH AIR AS POSSIBLE FROM BAG, SEAL, & FREEZE.

TO COOK AND ENJOY

1. THAW FREEZER MEAL OVERNIGHT IN REFRIGERATOR, OR IN MORNING IN WATER.
2. ADD CONTENTS OF FREEZER BAG TO CROCKPOT.
3. COOK ON "LOW" SETTING FOR 4 HOURS IN A 6-QUART CROCKPOT, OR 8 HOURS IN A 4-QUART.

NUTRITIONAL INFORMATION

SERVING SIZE: 1 1/3 CUPS
FAT: 15g
SODIUM: 1040mg
CARBS: 18g
SUGAR: 10g
PROTEIN: 33g

CILANTRO LIME CHICKEN

SERVES 6

INGREDIENTS

1/4 CUP FRESH CILANTRO

2 LBS BONELESS SKINLESS CHICKEN BREAST

4 TABLESPOONS UNSALTED BUTTER

1/4 TEASPOON SALT

1/4 TEASPOON PEPPER

1/4 TEASPOON CUMIN

JUICE & ZEST OF 1 LIME

TO FREEZE AND COOK LATER

1. LABEL YOUR FREEZER BAG WITH THE NAME OF THE RECIPE, COOKING INSTRUCTIONS, AND "USE BY" DATE (THREE MONTHS FROM WHEN YOU PREPPED THE MEAL).
2. ADD ALL INGREDIENTS TO YOUR FREEZER BAG.
3. REMOVE AS MUCH AIR AS POSSIBLE FROM BAG, SEAL, & FREEZE.

TO COOK AND ENJOY

1. THAW FREEZER MEAL OVERNIGHT IN REFRIGERATOR ,OR IN MORNING IN WATER.
2. ADD CONTENTS OF FREEZER BAG TO CROCKPOT.
3. COOK ON "LOW" SETTING FOR 4 HOURS IN A 6-QUART CROCKPOT, OR 8 HOURS IN A 4-QUART.
4. SHRED CHICKEN & MIX W/ JUICE REMAINING IN CROCKPOT.

NUTRITIONAL INFORMATION

SERVING SIZE: 1 CUP
FAT: 7g

SODIUM: 460mg
CARBS: 1g

SUGAR: 0g
PROTEIN: 32g

COOL RANCH SHREDDED CHICKEN TACOS

SERVES 6

INGREDIENTS

2 LBS BONELESS SKINLESS CHICKEN BREAST

2 TABLESPOONS RED WINE VINEGAR

3 TABLESPOONS OLIVE OIL

RANCH SEASONING PACKET

TACO SEASONING PACKET

(Make your own homemade seasoning packets from the recipe on page 200!)

TO FREEZE AND COOK LATER

1. LABEL YOUR FREEZER BAG WITH THE NAME OF THE RECIPE, COOKING INSTRUCTIONS, AND "USE BY" DATE (THREE MONTHS FROM WHEN YOU PREPPED THE MEAL).
2. ADD ALL INGREDIENTS TO YOUR FREEZER BAG.
3. REMOVE AS MUCH AIR AS POSSIBLE FROM BAG, SEAL, & FREEZE.

TO COOK AND ENJOY

1. THAW FREEZER MEAL OVERNIGHT IN REFRIGERATOR, OR IN MORNING IN WATER.
2. ADD CONTENTS OF FREEZER BAG TO CROCKPOT.
3. COOK ON "LOW" SETTING FOR 4 HOURS IN A 6-QUART CROCKPOT, OR 8 HOURS IN A 4-QUART.
4. SHRED CHICKEN & STIR.

NUTRITIONAL INFORMATION

SERVING SIZE: 1 CUP
SODIUM: 460mg
SUGAR: 1g
FAT: 12g
CARBS: 2g
PROTEIN: 33g

HONEY GARLIC CHICKEN

SERVES 6

INGREDIENTS

2 LBS BONELESS SKINLESS CHICKEN BREAST

1/2 CUP HONEY

1 TABLESPOON DIJON MUSTARD

6 CLOVES GARLIC, MINCED

1/2 CUP SOY SAUCE

1/4 CUP KETCHUP

1/2 TEASPOON SALT

1 TEASPOON PAPRIKA

1 TEASPOON CRUSHED RED PEPPER FLAKES

3 TABLESPOONS CORNSTARCH

TO FREEZE AND COOK LATER

1. LABEL YOUR FREEZER BAG WITH THE NAME OF THE RECIPE, COOKING INSTRUCTIONS, AND "USE BY" DATE (THREE MONTHS FROM WHEN YOU PREPPED THE MEAL).
2. ADD ALL INGREDIENTS TO YOUR FREEZER BAG.
3. REMOVE AS MUCH AIR AS POSSIBLE FROM BAG, SEAL, & FREEZE.

TO COOK AND ENJOY

1. THAW FREEZER MEAL OVERNIGHT IN REFRIGERATOR, OR IN MORNING IN WATER.
2. ADD CONTENTS OF FREEZER BAG TO CROCKPOT.
3. COOK ON "LOW" SETTING FOR 4 HOURS IN A 6-QUART CROCKPOT, OR 8 HOURS IN A 4-QUART.

NUTRITIONAL INFORMATION

SERVING SIZE: 1 CHICKEN BREAST
FAT: 0g
SODIUM: 870mg
CARBS: 30g
SUGAR: 24g
PROTEIN: 33g

ORANGE CHICKEN

INGREDIENTS

1/4 CUP LIGHT BROWN SUGAR

2 LBS BONELESS SKINLESS CHICKEN BREAST, CUT INTO BITE-SIZED PIECES

THE JUICE OF 2 LARGE NAVEL ORANGES

1/4 TABLESPOON CRUSHED RED PEPPER FLAKES

1 TABLESPOON SOY SAUCE

TO FREEZE AND COOK LATER

1. LABEL YOUR FREEZER BAG WITH THE NAME OF THE RECIPE, COOKING INSTRUCTIONS, AND "USE BY" DATE (THREE MONTHS FROM WHEN YOU PREPPED THE MEAL).
2. ADD ALL INGREDIENTS TO YOUR FREEZER BAG.
3. REMOVE AS MUCH AIR AS POSSIBLE FROM BAG, SEAL, & FREEZE.

TO COOK AND ENJOY

1. THAW FREEZER MEAL OVERNIGHT IN REFRIGERATOR, OR IN MORNING IN WATER.
2. ADD CONTENTS OF FREEZER BAG TO CROCKPOT.
3. COOK ON "LOW" SETTING FOR 4 HOURS IN A 6-QUART CROCKPOT, OR 8 HOURS IN A 4-QUART.

NUTRITIONAL INFORMATION

SERVING SIZE: 1 CUP
FAT: 0g
SODIUM: 500mg
CARBS: 5g
SUGAR: 2g
PROTEIN: 33g

THAI CHICKEN

INGREDIENTS

13.5oz CAN UNSWEETENED COCONUT MILK

1 TEASPOON CUMIN

2 LBS BONELESS SKINLESS CHICKEN BREAST

1 SMALL YELLOW ONION, DICED

1 LARGE GREEN BELL PEPPER, SLICED

THE JUICE & ZEST OF 2 LIMES

1 TEASPOON GROUND GINGER

1 TEASPOON CRUSHED RED PEPPER FLAKES

1 TEASPOON SALT

TO FREEZE AND COOK LATER

1. LABEL YOUR FREEZER BAG WITH THE NAME OF THE RECIPE, COOKING INSTRUCTIONS, AND "USE BY" DATE (THREE MONTHS FROM WHEN YOU PREPPED THE MEAL).
2. ADD ALL INGREDIENTS TO YOUR FREEZER BAG.
3. REMOVE AS MUCH AIR AS POSSIBLE FROM BAG, SEAL, & FREEZE.

TO COOK AND ENJOY

1. THAW FREEZER MEAL OVERNIGHT IN REFRIGERATOR, OR IN MORNING IN WATER.
2. ADD CONTENTS OF FREEZER BAG TO CROCKPOT.
3. COOK ON "LOW" SETTING FOR 4 HOURS IN A 6-QUART CROCKPOT, OR 8 HOURS IN A 4-QUART.
4. SHRED CHICKEN & STIR TO COMBINE.

NUTRITIONAL INFORMATION

SERVING SIZE: 1 1/3 CUPS
FAT: 1g
SODIUM: 500mg
CARBS: 5g
SUGAR: 2g
PROTEIN: 32g

ZESTY BBQ CHICKEN

INGREDIENTS

2 LBS BONELESS SKINLESS CHICKEN BREAST

1/2 CUP LIGHT BROWN SUGAR

2 TABLESPOONS APPLE CIDER VINEGAR

1 TEASPOON CHILI POWDER

1 TEASPOON ONION POWDER

1 TEASPOON GARLIC POWDER

1 TEASPOON BASIL

1/2 TEASPOON CRUSHED RED PEPPER FLAKES

1 TEASPOON OREGANO

TO FREEZE AND COOK LATER

1. LABEL YOUR FREEZER BAG WITH THE NAME OF THE RECIPE, COOKING INSTRUCTIONS, AND "USE BY" DATE (THREE MONTHS FROM WHEN YOU PREPPED THE MEAL).
2. ADD ALL INGREDIENTS TO YOUR FREEZER BAG.
3. REMOVE AS MUCH AIR AS POSSIBLE FROM BAG, SEAL, & FREEZE.

TO COOK AND ENJOY

1. THAW FREEZER MEAL OVERNIGHT IN REFRIGERATOR, OR IN MORNING IN WATER.
2. ADD CONTENTS OF FREEZER BAG TO CROCKPOT.
3. COOK ON "LOW" SETTING FOR 4 HOURS IN A 6-QUART CROCKPOT, OR 8 HOURS IN A 4-QUART.
4. SHRED CHICKEN & STIR TO COMBINE.

NUTRITIONAL INFORMATION

SERVING SIZE: 1 CUP
FAT: 0g
SODIUM: 550mg
CARBS: 29g
SUGAR: 27g
PROTEIN: 33g

CHICKEN & WILD RICE SOUP

SERVES 4

INGREDIENTS

1 LB BONELESS SKINLESS CHICKEN BREAST, FAT TRIMMED

1 TEASPOON BASIL

1/4 CUP WILD RICE, UNCOOKED

1 LB CARROTS, PEELED & DICED

1 SMALL YELLOW ONION, DICED

2 CELERY RIBS, CHOPPED

1/2 TEASPOON PEPPER

1/2 TEASPOON SALT

32oz CHICKEN BROTH (NOT NEEDED UNTIL DAY OF COOKING)

TO FREEZE AND COOK LATER

1. LABEL YOUR FREEZER BAG WITH THE NAME OF THE RECIPE, COOKING INSTRUCTIONS, AND "USE BY" DATE (THREE MONTHS FROM WHEN YOU PREPPED THE MEAL).
2. ADD ALL INGREDIENTS, EXCEPT BROTH, TO YOUR FREEZER BAG.
3. REMOVE AS MUCH AIR AS POSSIBLE FROM BAG, SEAL, & FREEZE.

TO COOK AND ENJOY

1. THAW FREEZER MEAL OVERNIGHT IN REFRIGERATOR, OR IN MORNING IN WATER.
2. ADD CONTENTS OF FREEZER BAG & BROTH TO CROCKPOT.
3. COOK ON "LOW" SETTING FOR 4 HOURS IN A 6-QUART CROCKPOT, OR 8-10 HOURS IN A 4-QUART.
4. SHRED CHICKEN & STIR.

NUTRITIONAL INFORMATION

SERVING SIZE: 1 CUP
FAT: 3g

SODIUM: 510mg
CARBS: 15g

SUGAR: 5g
PROTEIN: 19g

ITALIAN CHICKEN & QUINOA SOUP

SERVES 6

INGREDIENTS

1 LB BONELESS SKINLESS CHICKEN BREAST, FAT TRIMMED

5 OZ BAG BABY SPINACH

15oz CAN DARK RED KIDNEY BEANS, DRAINED & RINSED

28oz CAN DICED TOMATOES, UNDRAINED

1/4 CUP QUINOA, UNCOOKED

1/2 TEASPOON SALT

32oz CHICKEN BROTH (NOT NEEDED UNTIL DAY OF COOKING)

1 TABLESPOON ITALIAN SEASONING

TO FREEZE AND COOK LATER

1. LABEL YOUR FREEZER BAG WITH THE NAME OF THE RECIPE, COOKING INSTRUCTIONS, AND "USE BY" DATE (THREE MONTHS FROM WHEN YOU PREPPED THE MEAL).
2. ADD ALL INGREDIENTS, EXCEPT BROTH, TO YOUR FREEZER BAG.
3. REMOVE AS MUCH AIR AS POSSIBLE FROM BAG, SEAL, & FREEZE.

TO COOK AND ENJOY

1. THAW FREEZER MEAL OVERNIGHT IN REFRIGERATOR, OR IN MORNING IN WATER.
2. ADD CONTENTS OF FREEZER BAG & BROTH TO CROCKPOT.
3. COOK ON "LOW" SETTING FOR 4 HOURS IN A 6-QUART CROCKPOT, OR 8-10 HOURS IN A 4-QUART.
4. SHRED CHICKEN & STIR.

NUTRITIONAL INFORMATION

SERVING SIZE: 2 CUPS
FAT: 3g
SODIUM: 1200mg
CARBS: 24g
SUGAR: 6g
PROTEIN: 24g

LEMON CHICKEN W/ BABY SPINACH

INGREDIENTS

1 TABLESPOON PARSLEY

1/2 TEASPOON PEPPER

2 LBS BONELESS SKINLESS CHICKEN BREAST, FAST TRIMMED

1/4 CUP EXTRA VIRGIN OLIVE OIL

6 CLOVES GARLIC, MINCED

5oz BAG BABY SPINACH

THE JUICE OF 1 LEMON

1 TABLESPOON BASIL

1/2 TEASPOON SALT

TO FREEZE AND COOK LATER

1. LABEL YOUR FREEZER BAG WITH THE NAME OF THE RECIPE, COOKING INSTRUCTIONS, AND "USE BY" DATE (THREE MONTHS FROM WHEN YOU PREPPED THE MEAL).
2. ADD ALL INGREDIENTS TO YOUR FREEZER BAG.
3. REMOVE AS MUCH AIR AS POSSIBLE FROM BAG, SEAL, & FREEZE.

TO COOK AND ENJOY

1. THAW FREEZER MEAL OVERNIGHT IN REFRIGERATOR, OR IN MORNING IN WATER.
2. ADD CONTENTS OF FREEZER BAG TO CROCKPOT.
3. COOK ON "LOW" SETTING FOR 4 HOURS IN A 6-QUART CROCKPOT, OR 6-8 HOURS IN A 4-QUART.
4. SLICE OR SHRED CHICKEN & MIX W/ SPINACH AND SAUCE IN CROCKPOT.

NUTRITIONAL INFORMATION

SERVING SIZE: 1 CUP
FAT: 15g

SODIUM: 260mg
CARBS: 3g

SUGAR: 0g
PROTEIN: 34g

SHREDDED CHICKEN FAJITAS

SERVES 6

INGREDIENTS

2 LBS BONELESS SKINLESS CHICKEN BREAST, FAT TRIMMED

1 TABLESPOON CHILI POWDER

1/4 CUP EXTRA VIRGIN OLIVE OIL

1 RED BELL PEPPER, SLICED

1 GREEN BELL PEPPER, SLICED

1 RED ONION SLICED

THE JUICE OF 1 LIME

1/2 TEASPOON SALT

1 TEASPOON CRUSHED RED PEPPER FLAKES

2 TEASPOONS CUMIN POWDER

TO FREEZE AND COOK LATER

1. LABEL YOUR FREEZER BAG WITH THE NAME OF THE RECIPE, COOKING INSTRUCTIONS, AND "USE BY" DATE (THREE MONTHS FROM WHEN YOU PREPPED THE MEAL).
2. ADD ALL INGREDIENTS TO YOUR FREEZER BAG.
3. REMOVE AS MUCH AIR AS POSSIBLE FROM BAG, SEAL, & FREEZE.

TO COOK AND ENJOY

1. THAW FREEZER MEAL OVERNIGHT IN REFRIGERATOR, OR IN MORNING IN WATER.
2. ADD CONTENTS OF FREEZER BAG TO CROCKPOT.
3. COOK ON "LOW" SETTING FOR 4 HOURS IN A 6-QUART CROCKPOT, OR 6-8 HOURS IN A 4-QUART.
4. SHRED CHICKEN & RETURN TO CROCKPOT TO MIX W/ PEPPERS, ONIONS, & SAUCE.

NUTRITIONAL INFORMATION

SERVING SIZE: 1 CUP
FAT: 15g

SODIUM: 260mg
CARBS: 6g

SUGAR: 8g
PROTEIN: 34g

SPICY GARLIC LIME CHICKEN

SERVES 6

INGREDIENTS

2 LBS BONELESS SKINLESS CHICKEN BREAST, FAT TRIMMED

1/2 TEASPOON PEPPER

1/4 CUP EXTRA VIRGIN OLIVE OIL

1 SMALL YELLOW ONION, DICED

THE JUICE & ZEST OF 1 LIME

6 CLOVES GARLIC, MINCED

1 TEASPOON CRUSHED RED PEPPER FLAKES

TO FREEZE AND COOK LATER

1. LABEL YOUR FREEZER BAG WITH THE NAME OF THE RECIPE, COOKING INSTRUCTIONS, AND "USE BY" DATE (THREE MONTHS FROM WHEN YOU PREPPED THE MEAL).
2. ADD ALL INGREDIENTS TO YOUR FREEZER BAG.
3. REMOVE AS MUCH AIR AS POSSIBLE FROM BAG, SEAL, & FREEZE.

TO COOK AND ENJOY

1. THAW FREEZER MEAL OVERNIGHT IN REFRIGERATOR, OR IN MORNING IN WATER.
2. ADD CONTENTS OF FREEZER BAG TO CROCKPOT.
3. COOK ON "LOW" SETTING FOR 4 HOURS IN A 6-QUART CROCKPOT, OR 6-8 HOURS IN A 4-QUART.

NUTRITIONAL INFORMATION

SERVING SIZE: 1 CHICKEN BREAST
FAT: 15g
SODIUM: 230mg
CARBS: 4g
SUGAR: 1g
PROTEIN: 34g

CHICKEN CHILI

INGREDIENTS

1 LB BONELESS SKINLESS CHICKEN BREAST, FAT TRIMMED

15oz CAN CANNELLINI BEANS, DRAINED & RINSED

1 TABLESPOON CHILI POWDER

1 TABLESPOON PAPRIKA

14.5oz CAN PETITE DICED TOMATOES, UNDRAINED

1/4 TEASPOON CRUSHED RED PEPPER

1 RED PEPPER DICED

1.5 CUPS FROZEN CORN

4 CLOVES GARLIC, MINCED

14.5oz CAN DICED TOMATOES W/ GREEN CHILES, UNDRAINED

15oz CAN BLACK BEANS, DRAINED & RINSED

2 TEASPOONS GROUND CUMIN

1/2 TEASPOON OREGANO

TO FREEZE AND COOK LATER

1. LABEL YOUR FREEZER BAG WITH THE NAME OF THE RECIPE, COOKING INSTRUCTIONS, AND "USE BY" DATE (THREE MONTHS FROM WHEN YOU PREPPED THE MEAL).
2. ADD ALL INGREDIENTS TO YOUR FREEZER BAG.
3. REMOVE AS MUCH AIR AS POSSIBLE FROM BAG, SEAL, & FREEZE.

TO COOK AND ENJOY

1. THAW FREEZER MEAL OVERNIGHT IN REFRIGERATOR, OR IN MORNING IN WATER.
2. ADD CONTENTS OF FREEZER BAG TO CROCKPOT.
3. COOK ON "LOW" SETTING FOR 4 HOURS IN A 6-QUART CROCKPOT, OR 8 HOURS IN A 4-QUART.
4. SHRED CHICKEN & STIR.

NUTRITIONAL INFORMATION

SERVING SIZE: 1 2/3 CUP
FAT: 3.5g
SODIUM: 954mg
CARBS: 41g
SUGAR: 8g
PROTEIN: 35g

BBQ SHREDDED CHICKEN

SERVES 4

INGREDIENTS

1/2 TEASPOON ONION POWDER

1/2 TEASPOON GARLIC POWDER

1 LB BONELESS SKINLESS CHICKEN BREAST, FAT TRIMMED

3 TABLESPOONS APPLE CIDER

VINEGAR

2 TABLESPOONS DIJON MUSTARD

1/4 CUP LIGHT BROWN SUGAR

3/4 CUP KETCHUP

1/4 TEASPOON BLACK PEPPER

1 TEASPOON PAPRIKA

TO FREEZE AND COOK LATER

1. LABEL YOUR FREEZER BAG WITH THE NAME OF THE RECIPE, COOKING INSTRUCTIONS, AND "USE BY" DATE (THREE MONTHS FROM WHEN YOU PREPPED THE MEAL).
2. ADD ALL INGREDIENTS TO YOUR FREEZER BAG.
3. REMOVE AS MUCH AIR AS POSSIBLE FROM BAG, SEAL, & FREEZE.

TO COOK AND ENJOY

1. THAW FREEZER MEAL OVERNIGHT IN REFRIGERATOR OR IN MORNING IN WATER.
2. ADD CONTENTS OF FREEZER BAG TO CROCKPOT.
3. COOK ON "LOW" SETTING FOR 4 HOURS IN A 6-QUART CROCKPOT, OR 8 HOURS IN A 4-QUART.
4. SHRED CHICKEN & STIR.

NUTRITIONAL INFORMATION

SERVING SIZE: 1/2 CUP
FAT: 4g

SODIUM: 750mg
CARBS: 13g

SUGAR: 9g
PROTEIN: 44g

CHICKEN CHEESESTEAKS

INGREDIENTS

1 LB BONELESS SKINLESS CHICKEN BREAST, FAT TRIMMED

1 MEDIUM-SIZED GREEN BELL PEPPER, SLICED

1 SMALL YELLOW ONION, SLICED

1 TABLESPOON EXTRA VIRGIN OLIVE OIL

2 TEASPOONS APPLE CIDER VINEGAR

2 CLOVES GARLIC, MINCED

1 TABLESPOON HONEY

4 SLICES PROVOLONE CHEESE (NOT NEEDED UNTIL DAY OF COOKING)

2 MEDIUM-SIZED RED BELL PEPPERS, SLICED

TO FREEZE AND COOK LATER

1. LABEL YOUR FREEZER BAG WITH THE NAME OF THE RECIPE, COOKING INSTRUCTIONS, AND "USE BY" DATE (THREE MONTHS FROM WHEN YOU PREPPED THE MEAL).
2. ADD ALL INGREDIENTS, EXCEPT CHEESE, TO YOUR FREEZER BAG.
3. REMOVE AS MUCH AIR AS POSSIBLE FROM BAG, SEAL, & FREEZE.

TO COOK AND ENJOY

1. THAW FREEZER MEAL OVERNIGHT IN REFRIGERATOR, OR IN MORNING IN WATER.
2. ADD CONTENTS OF FREEZER BAG TO CROCKPOT.
3. COOK ON "LOW" SETTING FOR 4-6 HOURS IN A 6-QUART CROCKPOT, OR UNTIL CHICKEN IS COOKED THROUGH & TENDER.
4. CUT CHICKEN INTO SMALLER PIECES & SERVE ON ROLLS W/ COOKED PEPPERS, ONIONS, & MELTED PROVOLONE.

NUTRITIONAL INFORMATION

SERVING SIZE: 1 SUB
FAT: 15g

SODIUM: 340mg
CARBS: 13g

SUGAR: 9g
PROTEIN: 44g

CHICKEN TORTILLA SOUP

SERVES 6

INGREDIENTS

1 LB BONELESS SKINLESS CHICKEN BREAST, FAT TRIMMED

1 SMALL YELLOW ONION, CHOPPED

1 TABLESPOON CHILI POWDER

1/2 TEASPOON GROUND CUMIN

32oz LOW SODIUM CHICKEN BROTH (NOT NEEDED UNTIL DAY OF COOKING)

15oz CAN DICED MILD GREEN CHILES, UNDRAINED

15oz CAN BLACK BEANS

1.5 CUPS FROZEN CORN

4 CORN TORTILLAS, SLICED (NOT NEEDED UNTIL DAY OF COOKING)

1 MEDIUM RED BELL PEPPER, DICED

1/2 TEASPOON GARLIC POWDER

1/2 TEASPOON SALT

TO FREEZE AND COOK LATER

1. LABEL YOUR FREEZER BAG WITH THE NAME OF THE RECIPE, COOKING INSTRUCTIONS, AND "USE BY" DATE (THREE MONTHS FROM WHEN YOU PREPPED THE MEAL).
2. ADD ALL INGREDIENTS, EXCEPT BROTH & TORTILLAS, TO YOUR FREEZER BAG.
3. REMOVE AS MUCH AIR AS POSSIBLE FROM BAG, SEAL, & FREEZE.

TO COOK AND ENJOY

1. THAW FREEZER MEAL OVERNIGHT IN REFRIGERATOR, OR IN MORNING IN WATER.
2. ADD CONTENTS OF FREEZER BAG & BROTH TO CROCKPOT.
3. COOK ON "LOW" SETTING FOR 6-8 HOURS IN A 6-QUART CROCKPOT, OR UNTIL CHICKEN IS COOKED THROUGH & TENDER.
4. SHRED CHICKEN & RETURN TO CROCKPOT.
5. SERVE W/ SLICED CORN TORTILLAS FOR TOPPING.

NUTRITIONAL INFORMATION

SERVING SIZE: 1 2/3 CUPS
FAT: 4g
SODIUM: 790mg
CARBS: 33g
SUGAR: 6g
PROTEIN: 34g

HONEY DIJON CHICKEN

INGREDIENTS

2 LBS BONELESS SKINLESS CHICKEN BREAST, FAT TRIMMED

2 TABLESPOONS DIJON MUSTARD

1/4 CUP HONEY

2 TABLESPOONS BLACK PEPPER

1/2 TEASPOON SALT

1/2 TEASPOON GROUND THYME

1/2 CUP WATER (NOT NEEDED UNTIL DAY OF COOKING)

TO FREEZE AND COOK LATER

1. LABEL YOUR FREEZER BAG WITH THE NAME OF THE RECIPE, COOKING INSTRUCTIONS, AND "USE BY" DATE (THREE MONTHS FROM WHEN YOU PREPPED THE MEAL).
2. ADD ALL INGREDIENTS, EXCEPT WATER, TO YOUR FREEZER BAG.
3. REMOVE AS MUCH AIR AS POSSIBLE FROM BAG, SEAL, & FREEZE.

TO COOK AND ENJOY

1. THAW FREEZER MEAL OVERNIGHT IN REFRIGERATOR, OR IN MORNING IN WATER.
2. ADD CONTENTS OF FREEZER BAG & WATER TO CROCKPOT.
3. COOK ON "LOW" SETTING FOR 4-6 HOURS IN A 6-QUART CROCKPOT, OR UNTIL CHICKEN IS COOKED THROUGH & TENDER.

NUTRITIONAL INFORMATION

SERVING SIZE: 1 CHICKEN BREAST **SODIUM:** 430mg **SUGAR:** 11g
FAT: 5g **CARBS:** 12g **PROTEIN:** 48g

Recipe

Crockpot Lemon Pepper Chicken

Use by

12/18

Ingredients

Chicken breasts

Fresh lemon juice

EVOO

Salt & Pepper

Directions

Thaw.

Cook 3-6 hours on "low".

LEMON PEPPER CHICKEN

INGREDIENTS

2 LBS BONELESS SKINLESS CHICKEN BREAST, FAT TRIMMED

1/4 CUP EXTRA VIRGIN OLIVE OIL

THE JUICE OF 1 LEMON

1/2 TEASPOON PEPPER

1/4 TEASPOON SALT

TO FREEZE AND COOK LATER

1. LABEL YOUR FREEZER BAG WITH THE NAME OF THE RECIPE, COOKING INSTRUCTIONS, AND "USE BY" DATE (THREE MONTHS FROM WHEN YOU PREPPED THE MEAL).
2. ADD ALL INGREDIENTS TO YOUR FREEZER BAG.
3. REMOVE AS MUCH AIR AS POSSIBLE FROM BAG, SEAL, & FREEZE.

TO COOK AND ENJOY

1. THAW FREEZER MEAL OVERNIGHT IN REFRIGERATOR, OR IN MORNING IN WATER.
2. ADD CONTENTS OF FREEZER BAG TO CROCKPOT.
3. COOK ON "LOW" SETTING FOR 4-6 HOURS IN A 6-QUART CROCKPOT, OR UNTIL CHICKEN IS TENDER.

NUTRITIONAL INFORMATION

SERVING SIZE: 1 CHICKEN BREAST **SODIUM:** 210mg **SUGAR:** 0g
FAT: 15g **CARBS:** <1g **PROTEIN:** 48g

Chicken
Italian

ORANGE GINGER CHICKEN

INGREDIENTS

2 TABLESPOONS HONEY

2 LBS BONELESS SKINLESS CHICKEN BREAST, FAT TRIMMED

1/2" FRESH GINGER, PEELED & MINCED

THE JUICE OF 1 ORANGE

1 TEASPOON CRUSHED RED PEPPER FLAKES

2 TABLESPOONS COCONUT OIL

TO FREEZE AND COOK LATER

1. LABEL YOUR FREEZER BAG WITH THE NAME OF THE RECIPE, COOKING INSTRUCTIONS, AND "USE BY" DATE (THREE MONTHS FROM WHEN YOU PREPPED THE MEAL).
2. ADD ALL INGREDIENTS TO YOUR FREEZER BAG.
3. REMOVE AS MUCH AIR AS POSSIBLE FROM BAG, SEAL, & FREEZE.

TO COOK AND ENJOY

1. THAW FREEZER MEAL OVERNIGHT IN REFRIGERATOR, OR IN MORNING IN WATER.
2. ADD CONTENTS OF FREEZER BAG TO CROCKPOT.
3. COOK ON "LOW" SETTING FOR 4-6 HOURS IN A 6-QUART CROCKPOT, OR UNTIL CHICKEN IS TENDER.

NUTRITIONAL INFORMATION

SERVING SIZE: 1 CHICKEN BREAST **SODIUM:** 115mg **SUGAR:** 7g
FAT: 10g **CARBS:** 8g **PROTEIN:** 48g

RED PEPPER CHICKEN

SERVES 4

INGREDIENTS

1/4 CUP EXTRA VIRGIN OLIVE OIL

1/2 TEASPOON BLACK PEPPER

2 LBS BONELESS SKINLESS CHICKEN BREAST, FAT TRIMMED

1 MEDIUM RED BELL PEPPER, SLICED

1 SMALL YELLOW ONION, DICED

4 CLOVES GARLIC, MINCED

1 TEASPOON CRUSHED RED PEPPER

1/4 TEASPOON SALT

TO FREEZE AND COOK LATER

1. LABEL YOUR FREEZER BAG WITH THE NAME OF THE RECIPE, COOKING INSTRUCTIONS, AND "USE BY" DATE (THREE MONTHS FROM WHEN YOU PREPPED THE MEAL).
2. ADD ALL INGREDIENTS TO YOUR FREEZER BAG.
3. REMOVE AS MUCH AIR AS POSSIBLE FROM BAG, SEAL, & FREEZE.

TO COOK AND ENJOY

1. THAW FREEZER MEAL OVERNIGHT IN REFRIGERATOR, OR IN MORNING IN WATER.
2. ADD CONTENTS OF FREEZER BAG TO CROCKPOT.
3. COOK ON "LOW" SETTING FOR 4-6 HOURS IN A 6-QUART CROCKPOT, OR UNTIL CHICKEN IS TENDER.

NUTRITIONAL INFORMATION

SERVING SIZE: 1 CHICKEN BREAST
SODIUM: 210mg
SUGAR: 2g
FAT: 15g
CARBS: 4g
PROTEIN: 48g

SHREDDED BUFFALO CHICKEN

SERVES 4

INGREDIENTS

4 TABLESPOONS UNSALTED BUTTER

1 LB BONELESS SKINLESS CHICKEN BREAST, FAT TRIMMED

1 CUP HOT SAUCE

1/2 TEASPOON BLACK PEPPER

1 TEASPOON PAPRIKA

2 TABLESPOONS WHITE VINEGAR

TO FREEZE AND COOK LATER

1. LABEL YOUR FREEZER BAG WITH THE NAME OF THE RECIPE, COOKING INSTRUCTIONS, AND "USE BY" DATE (THREE MONTHS FROM WHEN YOU PREPPED THE MEAL).
2. ADD ALL INGREDIENTS TO YOUR FREEZER BAG.
3. REMOVE AS MUCH AIR AS POSSIBLE FROM BAG, SEAL, & FREEZE.

TO COOK AND ENJOY

1. THAW FREEZER MEAL OVERNIGHT IN REFRIGERATOR, OR IN MORNING IN WATER.
2. ADD CONTENTS OF FREEZER BAG TO CROCKPOT.
3. COOK ON "LOW" SETTING FOR 4-6 HOURS IN A 6-QUART CROCKPOT, OR UNTIL CHICKEN IS TENDER.
4. SHRED CHICKEN & MIX W/ REMAINING SAUCE IN CROCKPOT.

NUTRITIONAL INFORMATION

SERVING SIZE: 1/2 CUP
FAT: 15g

SODIUM: 2360mg
CARBS: 0g

SUGAR: 0g
PROTEIN: 36g

INDIAN BUTTER CHICKEN

INGREDIENTS

2 TEASPOONS ONION POWDER

4 CLOVES GARLIC, MINCED

2 LBS BONELESS SKINLESS CHICKEN THIGHS, CUT INTO BITE-SIZED PIECES

2-15oz CANS TOMATO SAUCE

16oz HEAVY WHIPPING CREAM

2 TABLESPOONS UNSALTED BUTTER

2 TABLESPOONS GARAM MASALA

2 TABLESPOONS CURRY POWDER

TO FREEZE AND COOK LATER

1. LABEL YOUR FREEZER BAG WITH THE NAME OF THE RECIPE, COOKING INSTRUCTIONS, AND "USE BY" DATE (THREE MONTHS FROM WHEN YOU PREPPED THE MEAL).
2. ADD ALL INGREDIENTS TO YOUR FREEZER BAG.
3. REMOVE AS MUCH AIR AS POSSIBLE FROM BAG, SEAL, & FREEZE.

TO COOK AND ENJOY

1. THAW FREEZER MEAL OVERNIGHT IN REFRIGERATOR, OR IN MORNING IN WATER.
2. ADD CONTENTS OF FREEZER BAG TO CROCKPOT.
3. COOK ON "LOW" SETTING FOR 4 HOURS IN A 6-QUART CROCKPOT, OR 8 HOURS IN A 4-QUART.

NUTRITIONAL INFORMATION

SERVING SIZE: 1 CUP
FAT: 36g
SODIUM: 900mg
CARBS: 15g
SUGAR: 5g
PROTEIN: 35g

ASIAN CHICKEN LETTUCE WRAPS

INGREDIENTS

2 LARGE CARROTS, GRATED

1/4 CUP KETCHUP

2 LBS GROUND CHICKEN

1 MEDIUM RED BELL PEPPER, DICED

1/4 CUP LOW-SODIUM SOY SAUCE

1/4 TEASPOON CRUSHED RED PEPPER FLAKES

4 CLOVES GARLIC, MINCED

1 TABLESPOON HONEY

TO FREEZE AND COOK LATER

1. LABEL YOUR FREEZER BAG WITH THE NAME OF THE RECIPE, COOKING INSTRUCTIONS, AND "USE BY" DATE (THREE MONTHS FROM WHEN YOU PREPPED THE MEAL).
2. ADD ALL INGREDIENTS TO YOUR FREEZER BAG.
3. REMOVE AS MUCH AIR AS POSSIBLE FROM BAG, SEAL, & FREEZE.

TO COOK AND ENJOY

1. THAW FREEZER MEAL OVERNIGHT IN REFRIGERATOR, OR IN MORNING IN WATER.
2. ADD CONTENTS OF FREEZER BAG TO CROCKPOT.
3. COOK ON "LOW" SETTING FOR 4-6 HOURS IN A 6-QUART CROCKPOT, OR UNTIL CHICKEN IS TENDER.
4. BREAK APART CHICKEN & SPOON ONTO LETTUCE WRAPS.

NUTRITIONAL INFORMATION

SERVING SIZE: 1/2 CUP
FAT: 11g
SODIUM: 600mg
CARBS: 11g
SUGAR: 7g
PROTEIN: 28g

TURKEY CHILI W/ BUTTERNUT SQUASH

SERVES 6

INGREDIENTS

2-15oz CANS BLACK BEANS, DRAINED& RINSED

1 TABLESPOON CHILI POWDER

1 LB GROUND TURKEY

1 LB BUTTERNUT SQUASH, PEELED & DICED

28oz CAN TOMATO SAUCE

1/2 TEASPOON CRUSHED RED PEPPER FLAKES

14.5oz CAN DICED TOMATOES, UNDRAINED

1 TABLESPOON GROUND CUMIN

TO FREEZE AND COOK LATER

1. LABEL YOUR FREEZER BAG WITH THE NAME OF THE RECIPE, COOKING INSTRUCTIONS, AND "USE BY" DATE (THREE MONTHS FROM WHEN YOU PREPPED THE MEAL).
2. ADD ALL INGREDIENTS TO YOUR FREEZER BAG.
3. REMOVE AS MUCH AIR AS POSSIBLE FROM BAG, SEAL, & FREEZE.

TO COOK AND ENJOY

1. THAW FREEZER MEAL OVERNIGHT IN REFRIGERATOR, OR IN MORNING IN WATER.
2. ADD CONTENTS OF FREEZER BAG TO CROCKPOT.
3. COOK ON "LOW" SETTING FOR 6 HOURS IN A 6-QUART CROCKPOT, OR 8-10 HOURS IN A 4-QUART.
4. BREAK APART TURKEY & STIR.

NUTRITIONAL INFORMATION

SERVING SIZE: 1 2/3 CUPS
FAT: 6g
SODIUM: 1040mg
CARBS: 45g
SUGAR: 11g
PROTEIN: 24g

GARDEN VEGETABLE SOUP W/ GROUND TURKEY

SERVES 6

INGREDIENTS

1 LB GROUND TURKEY

1 SMALL YELLOW ONION, DICED

2 CLOVES GARLIC, MINCED

1 TABLESPOON ITALIAN SEASONING

1/2 TEASPOON SALT

1/4 TEASPOON PEPPER

1/2 LB LARGE CARROTS, PEELED & CUT INTO BITE-SIZED PIECES

1 LB ZUCCHINI, CUT INTO BITE-SIZED PIECES

1 CAN CANNELLINI BEANS, DRAINED & RINSED

28oz CAN TOMATO SAUCE

1 TABLESPOON EXTRA VIRGIN OLIVE OIL

32oz LOW-SODIUM CHICKEN BROTH (NOT NEEDED UNTIL DAY OF COOKING)

TO FREEZE AND COOK LATER

1. LABEL YOUR FREEZER BAG WITH THE NAME OF THE RECIPE, COOKING INSTRUCTIONS, AND "USE BY" DATE (THREE MONTHS FROM WHEN YOU PREPPED THE MEAL).
2. ADD ALL INGREDIENTS, EXCEPT BROTH, TO YOUR FREEZER BAG.
3. REMOVE AS MUCH AIR AS POSSIBLE FROM BAG, SEAL, & FREEZE.

TO COOK AND ENJOY

1. THAW FREEZER MEAL OVERNIGHT IN REFRIGERATOR, OR IN MORNING IN WATER.
2. ADD CONTENTS OF FREEZER BAG & BROTH TO CROCK-POT.
3. COOK ON "LOW" SETTING FOR 8 HOURS, OR UNTIL TURKEY IS COOKED THROUGH & VEGETABLES TENDER.
4. BREAK APART TURKEY & STIR.

NUTRITIONAL INFORMATION

SERVING SIZE: 1 2/3 CUPS
FAT: 10g
SODIUM: 1190mg
CARBS: 29g
SUGAR: 9g
PROTEIN: 21g

Pork

BBQ BABY BACK RIBS

SERVES 5

INGREDIENTS

1 TABLESPOON CHILI POWDER

1 TEASPOON PAPRIKA

1 TEASPOON CURRY POWDER

3 LBS BABY BACK RIBS, CUT TO FIT INTO SLOW COOKER

1/4 CUP LIGHT BROWN SUGAR

2 TABLESPOONS WORCESTERSHIRE SAUCE

1 CUP KETCHUP

1/4 TEASPOON BLACK PEPPER

1/2 TEASPOON ONION POWDER

1/2 TEASPOON GARLIC POWDER

TO FREEZE AND COOK LATER

1. LABEL YOUR FREEZER BAG WITH THE NAME OF THE RECIPE, COOKING INSTRUCTIONS, AND "USE BY" DATE (THREE MONTHS FROM WHEN YOU PREPPED THE MEAL).
2. ADD ALL INGREDIENTS TO YOUR FREEZER BAG.
3. REMOVE AS MUCH AIR AS POSSIBLE FROM BAG, SEAL, & FREEZE.

TO COOK AND ENJOY

1. THAW FREEZER MEAL OVERNIGHT IN REFRIGERATOR, OR IN MORNING IN WATER.
2. ADD CONTENTS OF FREEZER BAG TO CROCKPOT.
3. COOK ON "LOW" SETTING FOR 6-8 HOURS IN A 6-QUART CROCKPOT, OR UNTIL RIBS ARE COOKED THROUGH & TENDER.
4. POUR RIBS ONTO A COOKIE SHEET COVERED W/ ALUMINUM FOIL.
5. BAKE FOR 15 MINUTES AT 350°F.

NUTRITIONAL INFORMATION

SERVING SIZE: THE MEAT OF 3-4 RIBS
FAT: 45g
SODIUM: 780mg
CARBS: 29g
SUGAR: 24g
PROTEIN: 30g

BBQ MAPLE RIBS

SERVES 6

INGREDIENTS

1 TABLESPOON CHILI POWDER

2 TEASPOONS CURRY POWDER

1 TEASPOON PEPPER

2 LBS BONELESS PORK RIBS

6oz CAN TOMATO PASTE

1/2 CUP PURE MAPLE SYRUP

2 TABLESPOONS APPLE CIDER VINEGAR

1 TEASPOON PAPRIKA

1 TEASPOON ONION POWDER

1 TEASPOON GARLIC POWDER

1/2 TEASPOON SALT

TO FREEZE AND COOK LATER

1. LABEL YOUR FREEZER BAG WITH THE NAME OF THE RECIPE, COOKING INSTRUCTIONS, AND "USE BY" DATE (THREE MONTHS FROM WHEN YOU PREPPED THE MEAL).
2. ADD ALL INGREDIENTS TO YOUR FREEZER BAG.
3. REMOVE AS MUCH AIR AS POSSIBLE FROM BAG, SEAL, & FREEZE.

TO COOK AND ENJOY

1. THAW FREEZER MEAL OVERNIGHT IN REFRIGERATOR, OR IN MORNING IN WATER.
2. ADD CONTENTS OF FREEZER BAG TO CROCKPOT.

COOK ON "LOW" SETTING FOR 6 HOURS IN A 6-QUART CROCKPOT, OR 8-10 HOURS IN A 4-QUART.

OPTIONAL: POUR CONTENTS OF CROCKPOT ONTO A COOKIE SHEET COVERED W/ ALUMINUM FOIL & BAKE FOR 15 MINUTES AT 350°F.

NUTRITIONAL INFORMATION

SERVING SIZE: 2 RIBS
FAT: 16g

SODIUM: 510mg
CARBS: 16g

SUGAR: 18g
PROTEIN: 44g

CRANBERRY PORK ROAST

SERVES 6

INGREDIENTS

3 LB BONE-IN PORK SHOULDER ROAST

15oz CAN WHOLE BERRY CRANBERRY SAUCE

1/4 CUP DRIED MINCED ONION

1/4 CUP HONEY

TO FREEZE AND COOK LATER

1. LABEL YOUR FREEZER BAG WITH THE NAME OF THE RECIPE, COOKING INSTRUCTIONS, AND "USE BY" DATE (THREE MONTHS FROM WHEN YOU PREPPED THE MEAL).
2. ADD ALL INGREDIENTS TO YOUR FREEZER BAG.
3. REMOVE AS MUCH AIR AS POSSIBLE FROM BAG, SEAL, & FREEZE.

TO COOK AND ENJOY

1. THAW FREEZER MEAL OVERNIGHT IN REFRIGERATOR, OR IN MORNING IN WATER.
2. ADD CONTENTS OF FREEZER BAG TO CROCKPOT.
3. COOK ON "LOW" SETTING FOR 6 HOURS IN A 6-QUART CROCKPOT, OR 8-10 HOURS IN A 4-QUART.
4. REMOVE BONES & SHRED MEAT.
5. SERVE W/ CRANBERRY SAUCE IN CROCKPOT.

NUTRITIONAL INFORMATION

SERVING SIZE: 1/2 CUP
FAT: 17g
SODIUM: 115mg
CARBS: 42g
SUGAR: 30g
PROTEIN: 34g

HONEY MUSTARD SESAME PORK ROAST

SERVES 6

INGREDIENTS

2 TABLESPOONS SESAME SEEDS

1 TEASPOON ONION POWDER

2 TABLESPOONS SESAME OIL

2 LBS BONELESS PORK ROAST

1/2 CUP SOY SAUCE

1/2 CUP HONEY

1/2 CUP WATER

1/4 TEASPOON CRUSHED RED PEPPER FLAKES

1/4 CUP DIJON MUSTARD

1/4 TEASPOON GARLIC POWDER

1/4 TEASPOON PEPPER

TO FREEZE AND COOK LATER

1. LABEL YOUR FREEZER BAG WITH THE NAME OF THE RECIPE, COOKING INSTRUCTIONS, AND "USE BY" DATE (THREE MONTHS FROM WHEN YOU PREPPED THE MEAL).
2. ADD ALL INGREDIENTS TO YOUR FREEZER BAG.
3. REMOVE AS MUCH AIR AS POSSIBLE FROM BAG, SEAL, & FREEZE.

TO COOK AND ENJOY

1. THAW FREEZER MEAL OVERNIGHT IN REFRIGERATOR, OR IN MORNING IN WATER.
2. ADD CONTENTS OF FREEZER BAG TO CROCKPOT.
3. COOK ON "LOW" SETTING FOR 6 HOURS IN A 6-QUART CROCKPOT, OR 8-10 HOURS IN A 4-QUART .
4. SHRED PORK & MIX W/ SAUCE IN CROCKPOT.

NUTRITIONAL INFORMATION

SERVING SIZE: 2/3 CUP
FAT: 13g
SODIUM: 70mg
CARBS: 37g
SUGAR: 23g
PROTEIN: 36g

MAPLE PORK ROAST W/ CINNAMON APPLESAUCE

SERVES 6

INGREDIENTS

2 LBS BONELESS PORK ROAST

2 LBS MCINTOSH APPLES, PEELED, CORED & CHOPPED

THE JUICE OF 1/2 A LEMON

2 TABLESPOONS PURE MAPLE SYRUP

1 TEASPOON CINNAMON

TO FREEZE AND COOK LATER

1. LABEL YOUR FREEZER BAG WITH THE NAME OF THE RECIPE, COOKING INSTRUCTIONS, AND "USE BY" DATE (THREE MONTHS FROM WHEN YOU PREPPED THE MEAL).
2. ADD APPLES & LEMON JUICE TO BAG & SEAL, SHAKE TO COMBINE.
3. OPEN FREEZER BAG & ADD REMAINING INGREDIENTS.
4. REMOVE AS MUCH AIR AS POSSIBLE FROM BAG, SEAL, & FREEZE.

TO COOK AND ENJOY

1. THAW FREEZER MEAL OVERNIGHT IN REFRIGERATOR, OR IN MORNING IN WATER.
2. ADD CONTENTS OF FREEZER BAG TO CROCKPOT.
3. COOK ON "LOW" SETTING FOR 6 HOURS IN A 6-QUART CROCKPOT, OR 8-10 HOURS IN A 4-QUART.
4. USING TWO FORKS, SHRED PORK.
5. SERVE W/ APPLESAUCE IN CROCKPOT.

NUTRITIONAL INFORMATION

SERVING SIZE: 2/3 CUP
FAT: 13g
SODIUM: 70mg
CARBS: 37g
SUGAR: 27g
PROTEIN: 32g

SWEET POTATO & PORK BURRITO BOWL

SERVES 6

INGREDIENTS

2 LARGE SWEET POTATOES, PEELED & CUBED

1 TABLESPOON CHILI POWDER

THE JUICE OF TWO LIMES

2 LBS BONELESS PORK ROAST, FAT TRIMMED

1 SMALL YELLOW ONION, SLICED

2 RED BELL PEPPERS, SLICED

3 CLOVES GARLIC, MINCED

1/2 TEASPOON CRUSHED RED PEPPER FLAKES

2 TEASPOONS GROUND CUMIN

1/2 TEASPOON SALT

TO FREEZE AND COOK LATER

1. LABEL YOUR FREEZER BAG WITH THE NAME OF THE RECIPE, COOKING INSTRUCTIONS, AND "USE BY" DATE (THREE MONTHS FROM WHEN YOU PREPPED THE MEAL).
2. ADD ALL INGREDIENTS TO YOUR FREEZER BAG.
3. REMOVE AS MUCH AIR AS POSSIBLE FROM BAG, SEAL, & FREEZE.

TO COOK AND ENJOY

1. THAW FREEZER MEAL OVERNIGHT IN REFRIGERATOR, OR IN MORNING IN WATER.
2. ADD CONTENTS OF FREEZER BAG TO CROCKPOT.
3. COOK ON "LOW" SETTING FOR 6 HOURS IN A 6-QUART CROCKPOT, OR 8-10 HOURS IN A 4-QUART.
4. SHRED PORK & SERVE W/ SWEET POTATOES, PEPPERS, & ONIONS IN CROCKPOT.

NUTRITIONAL INFORMATION

SERVING SIZE: 2/3 CUP
FAT: 13g
SODIUM: 310mg
CARBS: 16g
SUGAR: 5g
PROTEIN: 34g

MEDITERRANEAN SHREDDED PORK PITA POCKETS

SERVES 4

INGREDIENTS

1 TABLESPOON PAPRIKA

1 TABLESPOON ONION POWDER

1/2 TEASPOON BLACK PEPPER

2 LBS BONELESS PORK SHOULDER ROAST, FAT TRIMMED

2 TABLESPOONS EXTRA VIRGIN OLIVE OIL

2 CLOVES GARLIC, MINCED

1/2 TEASPOON SALT

2 TEASPOONS DRIED OREGANO

2 TEASPOONS DRIED BASIL

1 TEASPOONS DRIED ROSEMARY

TO FREEZE AND COOK LATER

1. LABEL YOUR FREEZER BAG WITH THE NAME OF THE RECIPE, COOKING INSTRUCTIONS, AND "USE BY" DATE (THREE MONTHS FROM WHEN YOU PREPPED THE MEAL).
2. ADD ALL INGREDIENTS TO YOUR FREEZER BAG.
3. REMOVE AS MUCH AIR AS POSSIBLE FROM BAG, SEAL, & FREEZE.

TO COOK AND ENJOY

1. THAW FREEZER MEAL OVERNIGHT IN REFRIGERATOR, OR IN MORNING IN WATER.
2. ADD CONTENTS OF FREEZER BAG TO CROCKPOT.
3. COOK ON "LOW" SETTING FOR 8 HOURS IN A 6-QUART CROCKPOT, OR UNTIL PORK IS COOKED THROUGH & TENDER.
4. SHRED PORK & SERVE AS PITA POCKETS.

NUTRITIONAL INFORMATION

SERVING SIZE: 2/3 CUP
FAT: 53g
SODIUM: 450mg
CARBS: 2g
SUGAR: 0g
PROTEIN: 38g

PARTY PORK ROAST

SERVES 6

INGREDIENTS

3 LB BONE-IN PORK SHOULDER ROAST

1 CUP GRAPE JELLY

1 CUP KETCHUP

1/4 TEASPOON GROUND ALLSPICE

TO FREEZE AND COOK LATER

1. LABEL YOUR FREEZER BAG WITH THE NAME OF THE RECIPE, COOKING INSTRUCTIONS, AND "USE BY" DATE (THREE MONTHS FROM WHEN YOU PREPPED THE MEAL).
2. ADD ALL INGREDIENTS TO YOUR FREEZER BAG.
3. REMOVE AS MUCH AIR AS POSSIBLE FROM BAG, SEAL, & FREEZE.

TO COOK AND ENJOY

1. THAW FREEZER MEAL OVERNIGHT IN REFRIGERATOR, OR IN MORNING IN WATER.
2. ADD CONTENTS OF FREEZER BAG TO CROCKPOT.
3. COOK ON "LOW" SETTING FOR 8 HOURS IN A 6-QUART CROCKPOT, OR UNTIL PORK IS COOKED THROUGH & TENDER.
4. REMOVE BONES & SHRED PORK.
5. STRAIN JUICE LEFT IN CROCKPOT & SERVE AS A GRAVY W/ MEAT.

NUTRITIONAL INFORMATION

SERVING SIZE: 2/3 CUP
FAT: 21g
SODIUM: 640mg
CARBS: 45g
SUGAR: 44g
PROTEIN: 31g

BBQ SHREDDED PORK

SERVES 8

INGREDIENTS

2 TABLESPOONS LIGHT BROWN SUGAR

2 TEASPOONS CURRY POWDER

2 BS BONELESS PORK ROAST, FAT TRIMMED

1 TABLESPOON CHILI POWDER

2 TABLESPOONS WORCHEST-SHIRE SAUCE

1 TEASPOON HOT SAUCE

TO FREEZE AND COOK LATER

1. LABEL YOUR FREEZER BAG WITH THE NAME OF THE RECIPE, COOKING INSTRUCTIONS, AND "USE BY" DATE (THREE MONTHS FROM WHEN YOU PREPPED THE MEAL).
2. ADD ALL INGREDIENTS TO YOUR FREEZER BAG.
3. REMOVE AS MUCH AIR AS POSSIBLE FROM BAG, SEAL, & FREEZE.

TO COOK AND ENJOY

1. THAW FREEZER MEAL OVERNIGHT IN REFRIGERATOR, OR IN MORNING IN WATER.
2. ADD CONTENTS OF FREEZER BAG TO CROCKPOT.
3. COOK ON "LOW" SETTING FOR 6-8 HOURS.
4. SHRED PORK & MIX W/ SAUCE IN CROCKPOT.

NUTRITIONAL INFORMATION

SERVING SIZE: 2/3 CUP
FAT: 31g
SODIUM: 650mg
CARBS: 15g
SUGAR: 12g
PROTEIN: 26g

PULLED PORK

SERVES 5

INGREDIENTS

1 TEASPOON GROUND CUMIN

1/2 TEASPOON GARLIC POWDER

3 LB BONELESS PORK SHOULDER ROAST, FAT TRIMMED

1 ONION, PEELED & HALVED

2 TABLESPOONS HONEY

2 TEASPOONS CHILI POWDER

1/4 TEASPOON BLACK PEPPER

1/2 TEASPOON SALT

TO FREEZE AND COOK LATER

1. LABEL YOUR FREEZER BAG WITH THE NAME OF THE RECIPE, COOKING INSTRUCTIONS, AND "USE BY" DATE (THREE MONTHS FROM WHEN YOU PREPPED THE MEAL).
2. ADD ALL INGREDIENTS TO YOUR FREEZER BAG.
3. REMOVE AS MUCH AIR AS POSSIBLE FROM BAG, SEAL, & FREEZE.

TO COOK AND ENJOY

1. THAW FREEZER MEAL OVERNIGHT IN REFRIGERATOR, OR IN MORNING IN WATER.
2. ADD CONTENTS OF FREEZER BAG TO CROCKPOT.
3. COOK ON "LOW" SETTING FOR 8 HOURS IN A 6-QUART CROCKPOT, OR UNTIL PORK IS COOKED THROUGH & TENDER.
4. SHRED PORK & SERVE.

NUTRITIONAL INFORMATION

SERVING SIZE: 1/2 CUP
FAT: 46g
SODIUM: 360mg
CARBS: 8g
SUGAR: 7g
PROTEIN: 38g

PEAR PORK TENDERLOIN

SERVES 6

INGREDIENTS

1 TEASPOON DRIED BASIL

1 TEASPOON BLACK PEPPER

2 LB BONELESS PORK TENDERLOIN

3 RIPE BOSC PEARS, PEELED & CUBED

3 CLOVES GARLIC, MINCED

1/4 CUP APPLE CIDER VINEGAR

1 TABLESPOON HONEY

1/2 TEASPOON ONION POWDER

1/2 TEASPOON SALT

TO FREEZE AND COOK LATER

1. LABEL YOUR FREEZER BAG WITH THE NAME OF THE RECIPE, COOKING INSTRUCTIONS, AND "USE BY" DATE (THREE MONTHS FROM WHEN YOU PREPPED THE MEAL).
2. ADD ALL INGREDIENTS TO YOUR FREEZER BAG.
3. REMOVE AS MUCH AIR AS POSSIBLE FROM BAG, SEAL, & FREEZE.

TO COOK AND ENJOY

1. THAW FREEZER MEAL OVERNIGHT IN REFRIGERATOR, OR IN MORNING IN WATER.
2. ADD CONTENTS OF FREEZER BAG TO CROCKPOT.
3. COOK ON "LOW" SETTING FOR 6 HOURS IN A 6-QUART CROCKPOT, OR 8-10 HOURS IN A 4-QUART.
4. SLICE & SHRED PORK, & SERVE W/ PEARS IN CROCKPOT.

NUTRITIONAL INFORMATION

SERVING SIZE: 1/2 CUP
FAT: 5g
SODIUM: 280mg
CARBS: 18g
SUGAR: 11g
PROTEIN: 38g

SWEET & SOUR GRAPE SHREDDED PORK

SERVES 6

INGREDIENTS

1 TEASPOON GARLIC POWDER

1/2 TEASPOON BLACK PEPPER

2 LB BONELESS PORK ROAST

1/2 CUP GRAPE JELLY

1/4 CUP SOY SAUCE

1/2 TEASPOON CRUSHED RED PEPPER FLAKES

1 TEASPOON ONION POWDER

1 TABLESPOON BALSAMIC VINEGAR

TO FREEZE AND COOK LATER

1. LABEL YOUR FREEZER BAG WITH THE NAME OF THE RECIPE, COOKING INSTRUCTIONS, AND "USE BY" DATE (THREE MONTHS FROM WHEN YOU PREPPED THE MEAL).
2. ADD ALL INGREDIENTS TO YOUR FREEZER BAG.
3. REMOVE AS MUCH AIR AS POSSIBLE FROM BAG, SEAL, & FREEZE.

TO COOK AND ENJOY

1. THAW FREEZER MEAL OVERNIGHT IN REFRIGERATOR, OR IN MORNING IN WATER.
2. ADD CONTENTS OF FREEZER BAG TO CROCKPOT.
3. COOK ON "LOW" SETTING FOR 6-8 HOURS IN A 6-QUART CROCKPOT.
4. SHRED PORK & MIX W/ SAUCE IN CROCKPOT.

NUTRITIONAL INFORMATION

SERVING SIZE: 1/2 CUP
FAT: 13g

SODIUM: 760mg
CARBS: 19g

SUGAR: 18g
PROTEIN: 34g

RANCH PORK CHOPS

SERVES 6

INGREDIENTS

1 TABLESPOON ONION POWDER

1/2 TEASPOON BLACK PEPPER

2 LBS BONELESS PORK CHOPS

3 TABLESPOONS EXTRA VIRGIN OLIVE OIL

2 TABLESPOONS RED WINE VINEGAR

1 TABLESPOON DRIED PARSLEY

1/2 TEASPOON DRIED DILL

1 TEASPOON GARLIC POWDER

1/2 TEASPOON SALT

TO FREEZE AND COOK LATER

1. LABEL YOUR FREEZER BAG WITH THE NAME OF THE RECIPE, COOKING INSTRUCTIONS, AND "USE BY" DATE (THREE MONTHS FROM WHEN YOU PREPPED THE MEAL).
2. ADD ALL INGREDIENTS TO YOUR FREEZER BAG.
3. REMOVE AS MUCH AIR AS POSSIBLE FROM BAG, SEAL, & FREEZE.

TO COOK AND ENJOY

1. THAW FREEZER MEAL OVERNIGHT IN REFRIGERATOR, OR IN MORNING IN WATER.
2. ADD CONTENTS OF FREEZER BAG TO CROCKPOT.
3. COOK ON "LOW" SETTING FOR 4-6 HOURS IN A 6-QUART CROCKPOT.

NUTRITIONAL INFORMATION

SERVING SIZE: 1 PORK CHOP
FAT: 20g
SODIUM: 270mg
CARBS: 2g
SUGAR: 1g
PROTEIN: 32g

CREAMY MUSHROOM PORK CHOPS

SERVES 6

INGREDIENTS

4oz MUSHROOMS, SLICED

1 TEASPOON ONION POWDER

1 TEASPOON GARLIC POWDER

2 LBS BONE-IN CENTER CUT PORK LOIN RIB EYE CHOPS

2 CUPS FROZEN PEAS

16oz HEAVY CREAM

1/2 CUP GRATED PARMESAN CHEESE

1/2 TEASPOON CELERY SEED

1/2 TEASPOON BLACK PEPPER

1/2 TEASPOON SALT

TO FREEZE AND COOK LATER

1. LABEL YOUR FREEZER BAG WITH THE NAME OF THE RECIPE, COOKING INSTRUCTIONS, AND "USE BY" DATE (THREE MONTHS FROM WHEN YOU PREPPED THE MEAL).
2. ADD ALL INGREDIENTS TO YOUR FREEZER BAG.
3. REMOVE AS MUCH AIR AS POSSIBLE FROM BAG, SEAL, & FREEZE.

TO COOK AND ENJOY

1. THAW FREEZER MEAL OVERNIGHT IN REFRIGERATOR, OR IN MORNING IN WATER.
2. ADD CONTENTS OF FREEZER BAG TO CROCKPOT.
3. COOK ON "LOW" SETTING FOR 6-8 HOURS IN A 6-QUART CROCKPOT.
4. SERVE W/ SAUCE IN CROCKPOT.

NUTRITIONAL INFORMATION

SERVING SIZE: 1 PORK CHOP
FAT: 45g
SODIUM: 430mg
CARBS: 10g
SUGAR: 2g
PROTEIN: 40g

ROSEMARY PORK LOIN

SERVES 6

INGREDIENTS

1 TABLESPOON ONION POWDER

1 TEASPOON GARLIC POWDER

2 LB BONELESS PORK LOIN

3 TABLESPOONS EXTRA VIRGIN OLIVE OIL

3 TABLESPOONS BALSAMIC VINEGAR

1 TABLESPOON ROSEMARY

1/2 TEASPOON BLACK PEPPER

1/2 TEASPOON SALT

TO FREEZE AND COOK LATER

1. LABEL YOUR FREEZER BAG WITH THE NAME OF THE RECIPE, COOKING INSTRUCTIONS, AND "USE BY" DATE (THREE MONTHS FROM WHEN YOU PREPPED THE MEAL).
2. ADD ALL INGREDIENTS TO YOUR FREEZER BAG.
3. REMOVE AS MUCH AIR AS POSSIBLE FROM BAG, SEAL, & FREEZE.

TO COOK AND ENJOY

1. THAW FREEZER MEAL OVERNIGHT IN REFRIGERATOR, OR IN MORNING IN WATER.
2. ADD CONTENTS OF FREEZER BAG TO CROCKPOT.
3. COOK ON "LOW" SETTING FOR 6-8 HOURS IN A 6-QUART CROCKPOT.
4. SLICE OR SHRED PORK & MIX W/ SAUCE IN CROCKPOT.

NUTRITIONAL INFORMATION

SERVING SIZE: 1/2 CUP
FAT: 12g
SODIUM: 292mg
CARBS: 3g
SUGAR: 2g
PROTEIN: 37g

EASY TUSCAN SAUSAGE

SERVES 5

INGREDIENTS

1 LB SWEET ITALIAN SAUSAGE

2 RED BELL PEPPERS, SLICED

1 SWEET YELLOW ONION, SLICED

15oz CAN TOMATO SAUCE

1 TABLESPOON ITALIAN SEASONING

TO FREEZE AND COOK LATER

1. LABEL YOUR FREEZER BAG WITH THE NAME OF THE RECIPE, COOKING INSTRUCTIONS, AND "USE BY" DATE (THREE MONTHS FROM WHEN YOU PREPPED THE MEAL).
2. ADD ALL INGREDIENTS TO YOUR FREEZER BAG.
3. REMOVE AS MUCH AIR AS POSSIBLE FROM BAG, SEAL, & FREEZE.

TO COOK AND ENJOY

1. THAW FREEZER MEAL OVERNIGHT IN REFRIGERATOR, OR IN MORNING IN WATER.
2. ADD CONTENTS OF FREEZER BAG TO CROCKPOT.
3. COOK ON "LOW" SETTING FOR 6-8 HOURS IN A 6-QUART CROCKPOT.

NUTRITIONAL INFORMATION

SERVING SIZE: 1 SAUSAGE & 1/2 CUP PEPPERS & ONIONS

FAT: 7g

SODIUM: 920mg

CARBS: 14g

SUGAR: 6g

PROTEIN: 15g

A Family Company
Une Entreprise Familiale
CROCKPOT SOUTHWESTERN CHICKEN CHILI
THAW. ADD TO CROCK WITH 2 CUPS WATER. COOK ON LOW FOR 4 HRS IN 6-QT OR 8 HRS IN 4-QUART CROCKPOT. SHRED CHICKEN
USE BY:
CROCKPOT HONEY LIME CHICKEN

FRENCH ONION PORK ROAST

SERVES 6

INGREDIENTS

1 TEASPOON ONION POWDER

1 TEASPOON CELERY SEED

2 LB BONELESS PORK ROAST, FAT TRIMMED

1 CUP BEEF BROTH

3 TABLESPOONS RED WINE VINEGAR

1 TEASPOON DRIED PARSLEY

1/4 CUP ONION FLAKES

1 TEASPOON PAPRIKA

1/2 TEASPOON BLACK PEPPER

TO FREEZE AND COOK LATER

1. LABEL YOUR FREEZER BAG WITH THE NAME OF THE RECIPE, COOKING INSTRUCTIONS, AND "USE BY" DATE (THREE MONTHS FROM WHEN YOU PREPPED THE MEAL).
2. ADD ALL INGREDIENTS TO YOUR FREEZER BAG.
3. REMOVE AS MUCH AIR AS POSSIBLE FROM BAG, SEAL, & FREEZE.

TO COOK AND ENJOY

1. THAW FREEZER MEAL OVERNIGHT IN REFRIGERATOR, OR IN MORNING IN WATER.
2. ADD CONTENTS OF FREEZER BAG TO CROCKPOT.
3. COOK ON "LOW" SETTING FOR 6-8 HOURS IN A 6-QUART CROCKPOT.
4. SHRED PORK & MIX W/ SAUCE IN CROCKPOT.

NUTRITIONAL INFORMATION

SERVING SIZE: 1/2 CUP
FAT: 13g
SODIUM: 210mg
CARBS: 3g
SUGAR: 1g
PROTEIN: 33g

ITALIAN SAUSAGE & PEPPERS

SERVES 5

INGREDIENTS

2 TABLESPOONS OLIVE OIL

1 TEASPOON DRIED BASIL

1 LB SWEET ITALIAN SAUSAGE

1 GREEN BELL PEPPER, SLICED

1 RED BELL PEPPER, SLICED

1 SWEET YELLOW ONION, SLICED

4 CLOVES GARLIC, MINCED

2 TABLESPOONS BALSAMIC VINEGAR

1 TEASPOON DRIED OREGANO

1 TEASPOON DRIED THYME

TO FREEZE AND COOK LATER

1. LABEL YOUR FREEZER BAG WITH THE NAME OF THE RECIPE, COOKING INSTRUCTIONS, AND "USE BY" DATE (THREE MONTHS FROM WHEN YOU PREPPED THE MEAL).
2. ADD ALL INGREDIENTS TO YOUR FREEZER BAG.
3. REMOVE AS MUCH AIR AS POSSIBLE FROM BAG, SEAL, & FREEZE.

TO COOK AND ENJOY

1. THAW FREEZER MEAL OVERNIGHT IN REFRIGERATOR, OR IN MORNING IN WATER.
2. ADD CONTENTS OF FREEZER BAG TO CROCKPOT.
3. COOK ON "LOW" SETTING FOR 6-8 HOURS IN A 6-QUART CROCKPOT.

NUTRITIONAL INFORMATION

SERVING SIZE: 1 SAUSAGE & 1/2 CUP PEPPERS & ONIONS

FAT: 13g

SODIUM: 760mg

CARBS: 9g

SUGAR: 4g

PROTEIN: 15g

JALAPEÑO LIME SHREDDED PORK TACOS

SERVES 6

INGREDIENTS

1 TABLESPOON HONEY

2 CLOVES GARLIC, MINCED

2 LB BONE-IN PORK SHOULDER ROAST

1 JALAPEÑO PEPPER, DESEEDED & SLICED

1 SMALL YELLOW ONION, DICED

THE JUICE OF TWO LIMES

1 TEASPOON CHILI POWDER

1/4 TEASPOON SALT

TO FREEZE AND COOK LATER

1. LABEL YOUR FREEZER BAG WITH THE NAME OF THE RECIPE, COOKING INSTRUCTIONS, AND "USE BY" DATE (THREE MONTHS FROM WHEN YOU PREPPED THE MEAL).
2. ADD ALL INGREDIENTS TO YOUR FREEZER BAG.
3. REMOVE AS MUCH AIR AS POSSIBLE FROM BAG, SEAL, & FREEZE.

TO COOK AND ENJOY

1. THAW FREEZER MEAL OVERNIGHT IN REFRIGERATOR, OR IN MORNING IN WATER.
2. ADD CONTENTS OF FREEZER BAG TO CROCKPOT.
3. COOK ON "LOW" SETTING FOR 8 HOURS IN A 6-QUART CROCKPOT, OR UNTIL PORK IS COOKED THROUGH & TENDER.
4. REMOVE BONE & SHRED PORK.
5. STRAIN JUICE LEFT IN CROCKPOT & MIX W/ MEAT.

OPTIONAL: SERVE ONIONS & PEPPERS ON TACOS TO ADD ADDITIONAL SPICE.

NUTRITIONAL INFORMATION

SERVING SIZE: 2/3 CUP
FAT: 31g

SODIUM: 210mg
CARBS: 7g

SUGAR: 4g
PROTEIN: 26g

ZUPPA TOSCANA W/ SWEET POTATOES

SERVES 6

INGREDIENTS

1 BUNCH KALE, CHOPPED

1.5 TEASPOONS FENNEL SEED

1.5 TEASPOONS PAPRIKA

1 LB GROUND SPICY ITALIAN

SAUSAGE

3 SWEET POTATOES, WASHED & SLICED

64oz CHICKEN BROTH (NOT NEEDED UNTIL DAY OF COOKING)

1 CUP HEAVY CREAM (NOT NEEDED UNTIL DAY OF COOKING)

1 TEASPOON BLACK PEPPER

1 TEASPOON ONION POWDER

1 TEASPOON GARLIC POWDER

TO FREEZE AND COOK LATER

1. LABEL YOUR FREEZER BAG WITH THE NAME OF THE RECIPE, COOKING INSTRUCTIONS, AND "USE BY" DATE (THREE MONTHS FROM WHEN YOU PREPPED THE MEAL).
2. ADD ALL INGREDIENTS, EXCEPT BROTH & CREAM, TO YOUR FREEZER BAG.
3. REMOVE AS MUCH AIR AS POSSIBLE FROM BAG, SEAL, & FREEZE.

TO COOK AND ENJOY

1. THAW FREEZER MEAL OVERNIGHT IN REFRIGERATOR, OR IN MORNING IN WATER.
2. ADD CONTENTS OF FREEZER BAG & BROTH TO CROCKPOT.
3. COOK ON "LOW" SETTING FOR 8 HOURS IN A 6-QUART CROCKPOT.
4. BREAK APART SAUSAGE & STIR IN HEAVY CREAM.

NUTRITIONAL INFORMATION

SERVING SIZE: 2 CUPS
FAT: 29g
SODIUM: 1350mg
CARBS: 19g
SUGAR: 4g
PROTEIN: 17g

SAUSAGE-STUFFED MINI SWEET PEPPERS

SERVES 6

INGREDIENTS

1.5 LBS MINI SWEET PEPPERS

1 LB GROUND SWEET ITALIAN SAUSAGE

24oz JAR MARINARA SAUCE

8oz MOZZARELLA CHEESE, SHREDDED (NOT NEEDED UNTIL DAY OF COOKING)

TO FREEZE AND COOK LATER

1. LABEL YOUR FREEZER BAG WITH THE NAME OF THE RECIPE, COOKING INSTRUCTIONS, AND "USE BY" DATE (THREE MONTHS FROM WHEN YOU PREPPED THE MEAL).
2. REMOVE TOPS OF PEPPERS & DESEED.
3. STUFF PEPPERS W/ SAUSAGE & ADD TO YOUR FREEZER BAG W/ MARINARA SAUCE.
4. REMOVE AS MUCH AIR AS POSSIBLE FROM BAG, SEAL, & FREEZE.

TO COOK AND ENJOY

1. THAW FREEZER MEAL OVERNIGHT IN REFRIGERATOR, OR IN MORNING IN WATER.
2. ADD CONTENTS OF FREEZER BAG TO CROCKPOT.
3. COOK ON "LOW" SETTING FOR 6-8 HOURS IN A 6-QUART CROCKPOT.
4. TOP WITH MOZZARELLA & COOK AN ADDITIONAL 10 MINUTES, OR UNTIL CHEESE IS MELTED.

NUTRITIONAL INFORMATION

SERVING SIZE: 1 CUP
FAT: 12g
SODIUM: 950mg
CARBS: 21g
SUGAR: 8g
PROTEIN: 21g

Veggie

COCONUT CHICKPEA CURRY

SERVES 6

INGREDIENTS

14.5oz CAN TOMATO SAUCE

6oz CAN TOMATO PASTE

1 SMALL YELLOW ONION, DICED

2 CLOVES GARLIC, MINCED

2-15oz CANS CHICKPEAS, DRAINED & RINSED

13.5oz CAN UNSWEETENED COCONUT MILK

1 TEASPOON CRUSHED RED PEPPER FLAKES

2 CUPS FROZEN PEAS

3 TABLESPOONS HONEY

2 TABLESPOONS CURRY POWDER

1 TEASPOON SALT

TO FREEZE AND COOK LATER

1. LABEL YOUR FREEZER BAG WITH THE NAME OF THE RECIPE, COOKING INSTRUCTIONS, AND "USE BY" DATE (THREE MONTHS FROM WHEN YOU PREPPED THE MEAL).
2. ADD ALL INGREDIENTS TO YOUR FREEZER BAG.
3. REMOVE AS MUCH AIR AS POSSIBLE FROM BAG, SEAL, & FREEZE.

TO COOK AND ENJOY

1. THAW FREEZER MEAL OVERNIGHT IN REFRIGERATOR, OR IN MORNING IN WATER.
2. ADD CONTENTS OF FREEZER BAG TO CROCKPOT.
3. COOK ON "LOW" SETTING FOR 4-6 HOURS IN A 6-QUART CROCKPOT.

NUTRITIONAL INFORMATION

SERVING SIZE: 2/3 CUP
FAT: 12g
SODIUM: 1180mg
CARBS: 47g
SUGAR: 21g
PROTEIN: 10g

RATATOUILLE

SERVES 6

INGREDIENTS

28oz CAN DICED TOMATOES, DRAINED

1 TABLESPOON FENNEL SEED

1 TABLESPOON BASIL

1 MEDIUM-SIZED EGGPLANT, PEELED & CUT LENGTHWISE INTO 4 PIECES

RAINBOW PACK BELL PEPPERS, CHOPPED

1 SMALL YELLOW ONION, DICED

4 CLOVES GARLIC, MINCED

15oz CAN CANNELLINI BEANS, DRAINED & RINSED

1/2 TEASPOON BLACK PEPPER

1/2 TEASPOON SALT

TO FREEZE AND COOK LATER

1. LABEL YOUR FREEZER BAG WITH THE NAME OF THE RECIPE, COOKING INSTRUCTIONS, AND "USE BY" DATE (THREE MONTHS FROM WHEN YOU PREPPED THE MEAL).
2. SPRINKLE CUT EGGPLANT W/ SALT, TOSS, & LET REST FOR 15 MINUTES TO REMOVE EXCESS MOISTURE. WIPE AWAY LIQUID & CUT INTO 1" SQUARES.
3. ADD ALL INGREDIENTS TO YOUR FREEZER BAG.
4. REMOVE AS MUCH AIR AS POSSIBLE FROM BAG, SEAL, & FREEZE.

TO COOK AND ENJOY

1. THAW FREEZER MEAL OVERNIGHT IN REFRIGERATOR, OR IN MORNING IN WATER.
2. ADD CONTENTS OF FREEZER BAG TO CROCKPOT.
3. COOK ON "LOW" SETTING FOR 4-6 HOURS IN A 6-QUART CROCKPOT, OR 8-10 HOURS IN A 4-QUART.

NUTRITIONAL INFORMATION

SERVING SIZE: 1 1/3 CUPS
FAT: 0g
SODIUM: 550mg
CARBS: 33g
SUGAR: 9g
PROTEIN: 6g

GARDEN VEGETABLE SOUP W/ PESTO

SERVES 6

INGREDIENTS

1/2 LB GREEN BEANS, ENDED & CHOPPED

2oz FRESH BABY SPINACH

1 SMALL ZUCCHINI, DICED

1 SMALL RED PEPPER, DICED

4 CLOVES GARLIC, MINCED

2-14.5oz CANS DICED TOMATOES, UNDRAINED

32oz VEGETABLE BROTH (NOT NEEDED UNTIL DAY OF COOKING)

6 TABLESPOONS PESTO (NOT NEEDED UNTIL DAY OF COOKING)

1/4 CUP PEARLED BARLEY (NOT FOR QUICK COOKING)

1 BAY LEAF

1 TABLESPOON LIGHT BROWN SUGAR

2 TABLESPOONS ITALIAN SEASONING

TO FREEZE AND COOK LATER

1. LABEL YOUR FREEZER BAG WITH THE NAME OF THE RECIPE, COOKING INSTRUCTIONS, AND "USE BY" DATE (THREE MONTHS FROM WHEN YOU PREPPED THE MEAL).
2. ADD ALL INGREDIENTS, EXCEPT BROTH & PESTO, TO YOUR FREEZER BAG.
3. REMOVE AS MUCH AIR AS POSSIBLE FROM BAG, SEAL, & FREEZE.

TO COOK AND ENJOY

1. THAW FREEZER MEAL OVERNIGHT IN REFRIGERATOR, OR IN MORNING IN WATER.
2. ADD CONTENTS OF FREEZER BAG & BROTH TO CROCKPOT.
3. COOK ON "LOW" SETTING FOR 6 HOURS IN A 6-QUART CROCKPOT, OR 8-10 HOURS IN A 4-QUART.
4. REMOVE BAY LEAF & SPOON INTO BOWLS WITH PESTO.

NUTRITIONAL INFORMATION

SERVING SIZE: 2 CUPS
FAT: 7g
SODIUM: 1040mg
CARBS: 32g
SUGAR: 10g
PROTEIN: 6g

SIMPLE LASAGNA SOUP

SERVES 6

INGREDIENTS

4 CUPS CHICKEN BROTH (NOT NEEDED UNTIL DAY OF COOKING)

24oz JAR MARINARA SAUCE

3 UNCOOKED LASAGNA NOODLES, BROKEN INTO SMALL PIECES (NOT NEEDED UNTIL DAY OF COOKING)

3 CUPS FRESH BABY SPINACH

15oz CAN CANNELLINI BEANS, DRAINED & RINSED

TO FREEZE AND COOK LATER

1. LABEL YOUR FREEZER BAG WITH THE NAME OF THE RECIPE, COOKING INSTRUCTIONS, AND "USE BY" DATE (THREE MONTHS FROM WHEN YOU PREPPED THE MEAL).
2. ADD ALL INGREDIENTS, EXCEPT BROTH & NOODLES, TO YOUR FREEZER BAG.
3. REMOVE AS MUCH AIR AS POSSIBLE FROM BAG, SEAL, & FREEZE.

TO COOK AND ENJOY

1. THAW FREEZER MEAL OVERNIGHT IN REFRIGERATOR, OR IN MORNING IN WATER.
2. ADD CONTENTS OF FREEZER BAG & BROTH TO CROCK-POT.
3. COOK ON "LOW" SETTING FOR 6-8 HOURS IN A 6-QUART CROCKPOT.
4. ADD BROKEN LASAGNA NOODLES & COOK FOR AN ADDITIONAL 30 MINUTES.

NUTRITIONAL INFORMATION

SERVING SIZE: 1 1/3 CUPS
FAT: 2g
SODIUM: 880mg
CARBS: 31g
SUGAR: 9g
PROTEIN: 8g

BLACK BEAN ENCHILADA STACK

SERVES 6

INGREDIENTS

8 SMALL CORN TORTILLAS, SLICED INTO 8 PIECES EACH

1 TEASPOON GARLIC SALT

4 TEASPOONS CHILI POWDER

4-15oz CANS BLACK BEANS, DRAINED & RINSED

2-10oz CANS DICED TOMATOES W/ GREEN CHILES

1 SMALL YELLOW ONION, DICED

8oz SHREDDED SHARP CHEDDAR CHEESE

4 TEASPOONS GROUND CUMIN

TO FREEZE AND COOK LATER

1. LABEL YOUR FREEZER BAG WITH THE NAME OF THE RECIPE, COOKING INSTRUCTIONS, AND "USE BY" DATE (THREE MONTHS FROM WHEN YOU PREPPED THE MEAL).
2. ADD CHEESE TO QUART-SIZED BAG. LABEL, SEAL, & FREEZE.
3. IN A LARGE BOWL, COMBINE ALL REMAINING INGREDIENTS, EXCEPT TORTILLAS.
4. FILL GALLON-SIZED BAG W/ TORTILLAS, FOLLOWED BY BLACK BEAN MIXTURE.
5. REMOVE AS MUCH AIR AS POSSIBLE FROM BAG, SEAL, & FREEZE.

TO COOK AND ENJOY

1. THAW FREEZER MEAL OVERNIGHT IN REFRIGERATOR, OR IN MORNING IN WATER.
2. ADD CONTENTS OF GALLON-SIZED FREEZER BAG TO CROCKPOT.
3. COOK ON "LOW" SETTING FOR 6-8 HOURS IN A 6-QUART CROCKPOT.
4. TOP W/ SHREDDED CHEESE & COOK AN ADDITIONAL 15 MINUTES, OR UNTIL CHEESE IS MELTED.

NUTRITIONAL INFORMATION

SERVING SIZE: 1 PIECE
FAT: 13g
SODIUM: 1440mg
CARBS: 66g
SUGAR: 10g
PROTEIN: 32g

CHEESY EGGPLANT BAKE

SERVES 6

INGREDIENTS

1/2 CUP SHREDDED PARMESAN CHEESE

1/2 CUP PASTA SAUCE

2 EGGS

8oz MOZZARELLA CHEESE, FRESHLY SHREDDED, DIVIDED IN HALF

1 LARGE EGGPLANT, ENDS CUT OFF & THINLY SLICED INTO ROUNDS

15oz CONTAINER PART-SKIM RICOTTA CHEESE

1 TABLESPOON DRIED PARSLEY FLAKES

1/2 TEASPOON BLACK PEPPER

3/4 TEASPOON SALT

TO FREEZE AND COOK LATER

1. ADD HALF OF MOZZARELLA CHEESE TO A QUART-SIZED BAG. LABEL, SEAL, & FREEZE.
2. LABEL YOUR FREEZER BAG WITH THE NAME OF THE RECIPE, COOKING INSTRUCTIONS, AND "USE BY" DATE (THREE MONTHS FROM WHEN YOU PREPPED THE MEAL).
3. IN A LARGE BOWL, COMBINE ALL REMAINING HALF OF MOZZARELLA W/ RICOTTA, PARMESAN, EGGS, PARSLEY FLAKES, SALT & PEPPER.
4. FILL GALLON-SIZED BAG W/ EGGPLANT ROUNDS FOLLOWED BY CHEESE MIXTURE & PASTA SAUCE
5. REMOVE AS MUCH AIR AS POSSIBLE FROM BAG, SEAL, & FREEZE.

TO COOK AND ENJOY

1. THAW FREEZER MEAL OVERNIGHT IN REFRIGERATOR, OR IN MORNING IN WATER.
2. ADD CONTENTS OF GALLON-SIZED FREEZER BAG TO CROCKPOT.
3. COOK ON "LOW" SETTING FOR 6-8 HOURS IN A 6-QUART CROCKPOT.
4. TOP W/ SHREDDED CHEESE & COOK AN ADDITIONAL 15 MINUTES, OR UNTIL CHEESE IS MELTED.

NUTRITIONAL INFORMATION

SERVING SIZE: 1 PIECE
FAT: 17g
SODIUM: 830mg
CARBS: 11g
SUGAR: 4g
PROTEIN: 24g

MEXICAN STUFFED PEPPERS

SERVES 6

INGREDIENTS

15oz CAN BLACK BEANS, DRAINED & RINSED

1 TABLESPOON HONEY

1 TABLESPOON CHILI POWDER

6 RED BELL PEPPERS

1 SMALL YELLOW ONION, DICED

8oz FROZEN CORN

THE JUICE & ZEST OF ONE LIME

1/4 TEASPOON CRUSHED RED PEPPER FLAKES

1 TEASPOON GROUND CUMIN

1/2 TEASPOON GARLIC SALT

TO FREEZE AND COOK LATER

1. LABEL YOUR FREEZER BAG WITH THE NAME OF THE RECIPE, COOKING INSTRUCTIONS, AND "USE BY" DATE (THREE MONTHS FROM WHEN YOU PREPPED THE MEAL).
2. IN A LARGE BOWL, COMBINE ALL REMAINING INGREDIENTS, EXCEPT PEPPERS.
3. SLICE OFF THE VERY TOPS OF PEPPERS & CLEAN. DICE TOPS & ADD TO BLACK BEAN MIXTURE.
4. STUFF EACH PEPPER W/ 3/4 CUP MIXTURE.
5. ADD TO FREEZER BAG & FREEZE.

TO COOK AND ENJOY

1. THAW FREEZER MEAL OVERNIGHT IN REFRIGERATOR, OR IN MORNING IN WATER.
2. ADD PEPPERS TO CROCKPOT.
3. COOK ON "LOW" SETTING FOR 6-8 HOURS IN A 6-QUART CROCKPOT.

NUTRITIONAL INFORMATION

SERVING SIZE: 1 STUFFED PEPPER
FAT: 1g
SODIUM: 290mg
CARBS: 36g
SUGAR: 12g
PROTEIN: 8g

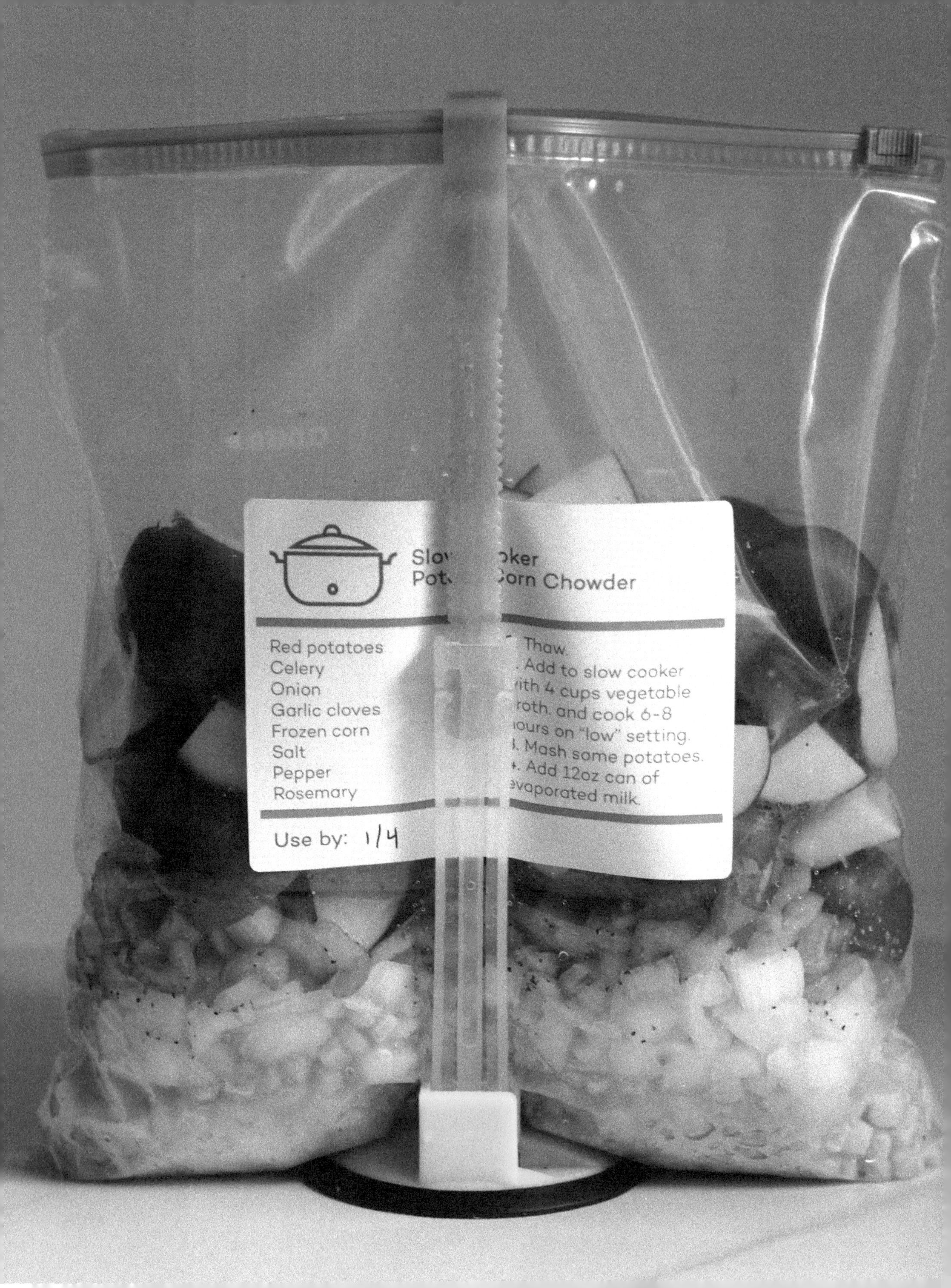

Corn Chowder
Red potatoes
Celery
Onion
Garlic cloves
Frozen corn
Salt
Pepper
Rosemary
Thaw.
Add to slow cooker
4 cups vegetable
and cook 6-8
on "low" setting.
Mash some potatoes.
Add 12oz can of
milk.
Use by: 1/4

POTATO & CORN CHOWDER

SERVES 6

INGREDIENTS

4 CUPS VEGETABLE BROTH (NOT NEEDED UNTIL DAY OF COOKING)

8oz FROZEN CORN

1/2 TEASPOON BLACK PEPPER

1 TEASPOON DRIED ROSEMARY

3 LBS RED POTATOES, CUT INTO 1" PIECES

4 RIBS OF CELERY, DICED

1 SMALL YELLOW ONION, DICED

4 CLOVES GARLIC, MINCED

12oz CAN VITAMIN D EVAPORATED MILK (NOT NEEDED UNTIL DAY OF COOKING)

1 TEASPOON SALT

TO FREEZE AND COOK LATER

1. LABEL YOUR FREEZER BAG WITH THE NAME OF THE RECIPE, COOKING INSTRUCTIONS, AND "USE BY" DATE (THREE MONTHS FROM WHEN YOU PREPPED THE MEAL).
2. ADD ALL INGREDIENTS, EXCEPT BROTH & EVAPORATED MILK, TO FREEZER BAG.
3. REMOVE AS MUCH AIR AS POSSIBLE FROM BAG, SEAL, & FREEZE.

TO COOK AND ENJOY

1. THAW FREEZER MEAL OVERNIGHT IN REFRIGERATOR, OR IN MORNING IN WATER.
2. ADD CONTENTS OF FREEZER BAG & BROTH TO CROCKPOT.
3. COOK ON "LOW" SETTING FOR 6-8 HOURS IN A 6-QUART CROCKPOT.
4. ADD EVAPORATED MILK & COOK AN ADDITIONAL 10 MINUTES, OR UNTIL HEATED THROUGH.

NUTRITIONAL INFORMATION

SERVING SIZE: 2 CUPS
FAT: 5g

SODIUM: 1130mg
CARBS: 62g

SUGAR: 8g
PROTEIN: 10g

THAI PINEAPPLE CURRY

SERVES 6

INGREDIENTS

13.5oz CAN UNSWEETENED COCONUT MILK

1 GREEN BELL PEPPER, SLICED

1 SMALL YELLOW ONION, CHOPPED

2 CLOVES GARLIC, MINCED

15oz CAN CHICKPEAS, DRAINED & RINSED

1 FRESH PINEAPPLE, CORED & CHOPPED INTO 1" PIECES

1 LB SWEET POTATOES, PEELED & CUT INTO 1" PIECES

1/2 TEASPOON CRUSHED RED PEPPER FLAKES

3 TABLESPOONS CURRY POWDER

1.5 TEASPOONS SALT

TO FREEZE AND COOK LATER

1. LABEL YOUR FREEZER BAG WITH THE NAME OF THE RECIPE, COOKING INSTRUCTIONS, AND "USE BY" DATE (THREE MONTHS FROM WHEN YOU PREPPED THE MEAL).
2. ADD ALL INGREDIENTS TO FREEZER BAG.
3. REMOVE AS MUCH AIR AS POSSIBLE FROM BAG, SEAL, & FREEZE.

TO COOK AND ENJOY

1. THAW FREEZER MEAL OVERNIGHT IN REFRIGERATOR, OR IN MORNING IN WATER.
2. ADD CONTENTS OF FREEZER BAG TO CROCKPOT.
3. COOK ON "LOW" SETTING FOR 6-8 HOURS IN A 6-QUART CROCKPOT, OR UNTIL PEPPERS & ONIONS ARE TENDER.

NUTRITIONAL INFORMATION

SERVING SIZE: 1 CUP
FAT: 2g
SODIUM: 750mg
CARBS: 45g
SUGAR: 22g
PROTEIN: 5g

THREE BEAN CHILI

SERVES 6

INGREDIENTS

14.5oz CAN DICED TOMATOES, UNDRAINED

28oz CAN TOMATO SAUCE

4 CLOVES GARLIC, MINCED

2 TABLESPOONS LIGHT BROWN SUGAR

2-15oz CANS RED KIDNEY BEANS, DRAINED & RINSED

15oz CAN PINTO BEANS, DRAINED & RINSED

15oz CAN BLACK BEANS, DRAINED & RINSED

1/4 TEASPOON CRUSHED RED PEPPER FLAKES

1 TABLESPOON CHILI POWDER

2 TEASPOONS GROUND CUMIN

1 CUP WATER (NOT NEEDED UNTIL DAY OF COOKING)

TO FREEZE AND COOK LATER

1. LABEL YOUR FREEZER BAG WITH THE NAME OF THE RECIPE, COOKING INSTRUCTIONS, AND "USE BY" DATE (THREE MONTHS FROM WHEN YOU PREPPED THE MEAL).
2. ADD ALL INGREDIENTS, EXCEPT WATER, TO FREEZER BAG.
3. REMOVE AS MUCH AIR AS POSSIBLE FROM BAG, SEAL, & FREEZE.

TO COOK AND ENJOY

1. THAW FREEZER MEAL OVERNIGHT IN REFRIGERATOR, OR IN MORNING IN WATER.
2. ADD CONTENTS OF FREEZER BAG & WATER TO CROCKPOT.
3. COOK ON "LOW" SETTING FOR 6-8 HOURS IN A 6-QUART CROCKPOT.

NUTRITIONAL INFORMATION

SERVING SIZE: 1 1/3 CUPS
FAT: 9g
SODIUM: 1470mg
CARBS: 74g
SUGAR: 13g
PROTEIN: 20g

TUSCAN TORTELLINI SOUP

SERVES 6

INGREDIENTS

19oz BAG FROZEN CHEESE TORTELLINI (NOT NEEDED UNTIL DAY OF COOKING)

1 SMALL YELLOW ONION, DICED

24oz JAR PASTA SAUCE

15oz CAN CANNELLINI BEANS, DRAINED & RINSED

8 LARGE CARROTS, PEELED & DICED

1/2 LB FRESH GREEN BEANS, ENDS CUT OFF & CUT INTO 1" PIECES

32oz VEGETABLE BROTH (NOT NEEDED UNTIL DAY OF COOKING)

5oz FRESH BABY SPINACH

TO FREEZE AND COOK LATER

1. LABEL YOUR FREEZER BAG WITH THE NAME OF THE RECIPE, COOKING INSTRUCTIONS, AND "USE BY" DATE (THREE MONTHS FROM WHEN YOU PREPPED THE MEAL).
2. ADD ALL INGREDIENTS, EXCEPT BROTH & TORTELLINI, TO FREEZER BAG.
3. REMOVE AS MUCH AIR AS POSSIBLE FROM BAG, SEAL, & FREEZE.

TO COOK AND ENJOY

1. THAW FREEZER MEAL OVERNIGHT IN REFRIGERATOR, OR IN MORNING IN WATER.
2. ADD CONTENTS OF FREEZER BAG & BROTH TO CROCKPOT.
3. COOK ON "LOW" SETTING FOR 6-8 HOURS IN A 6-QUART CROCKPOT, OR UNTIL CARROTS & ONIONS ARE SOFT.
4. ADD TORTELLINI & COOK AN ADDITIONAL 15 MINUTES ON HIGH.

NUTRITIONAL INFORMATION

SERVING SIZE: 1 2/3 CUPS
FAT: 9g
SODIUM: 1470mg
CARBS: 74g
SUGAR: 13g
PROTEIN: 20g

CREAMY POTATO SOUP

SERVES 8

INGREDIENTS

12oz CAN EVAPORATED MILK W/ VITAMIN A (NOT NEEDED UNTIL DAY OF COOKING)

8oz FROZEN BROCCOLI FLORETS

1/2 TEASPOON BLACK PEPPER

3 LBS RUSSET POTATOES, PEELED & CUT INTO 1" CHUNKS

4 MEDIUM-SIZED CELERY STALKS, DICED

2 SMALL YELLOW ONIONS, DICED

4 CLOVES GARLIC, MINCED

4 CUPS LOW-SODIUM CHICKEN BROTH (NOT NEEDED UNTIL DAY OF COOKING)

4 CUPS WATER (NOT NEEDED UNTIL DAY OF COOKING)

TO FREEZE AND COOK LATER

1. LABEL YOUR FREEZER BAG WITH THE NAME OF THE RECIPE, COOKING INSTRUCTIONS, AND "USE BY" DATE (THREE MONTHS FROM WHEN YOU PREPPED THE MEAL).
2. ADD ALL INGREDIENTS, EXCEPT BROTH, WATER & EVAPORATED MILK, TO FREEZER BAG.
3. REMOVE AS MUCH AIR AS POSSIBLE FROM BAG, SEAL, & FREEZE.

TO COOK AND ENJOY

1. ADD FROZEN CONTENTS OF FREEZER BAG TO CROCKPOT.
2. COOK ON "LOW" SETTING FOR 8 HOURS IN A 6-QUART CROCKPOT, OR UNTIL POTATOES ARE SOFT.
3. STIR IN EVAPORATED MILK & CONTINUE TO COOK FOR 5 MINUTES, OR UNTIL HEATED THROUGH.

NUTRITIONAL INFORMATION

SERVING SIZE: 2 CUPS
FAT: 5g
SODIUM: 160mg
CARBS: 52g
SUGAR: 4g
PROTEIN: 14g

GREENS & BEANS

SERVES 6

INGREDIENTS

1 HEAD ESCAROLE, THINLY SLICED

5oz BABY SPINACH

6 CLOVES GARLIC, MINCED

2-15oz CANS CANNELLINI BEANS, DRAINED & RINSED

32oz VEGETABLE BROTH (NOT NEEDED UNTIL DAY OF COOKING)

1 TABLESPOON OLIVE OIL

1/2 TEASPOON SALT

3/4 TEASPOON BLACK PEPPER

TO FREEZE AND COOK LATER

1. LABEL YOUR FREEZER BAG WITH THE NAME OF THE RECIPE, COOKING INSTRUCTIONS, AND "USE BY" DATE (THREE MONTHS FROM WHEN YOU PREPPED THE MEAL).
2. ADD ALL INGREDIENTS EXCEPT BROTH TO FREEZER BAG.
3. REMOVE AS MUCH AIR AS POSSIBLE FROM BAG, SEAL, & FREEZE.

TO COOK AND ENJOY

1. THAW FREEZER MEAL OVERNIGHT IN REFRIGERATOR, OR IN MORNING IN WATER.
2. ADD CONTENTS OF FREEZER BAG TO CROCKPOT.
3. COOK ON "LOW" SETTING FOR 4-6 HOURS IN A 6-QUART CROCKPOT.

NUTRITIONAL INFORMATION

SERVING SIZE: 1 1/2 CUPS
FAT: 3g
SODIUM: 980mg
CARBS: 28g
SUGAR: 2g
PROTEIN: 10g

LENTIL SLOPPY JOES

SERVES 8

INGREDIENTS

1 TABLESPOON LIGHT BROWN SUGAR

1 TABLESPOON CHILI POWDER

1/2 TEASPOON GARLIC POWDER

2 CUPS VEGETABLE BROTH

2 CUPS DRIED UNCOOKED LENTILS, RINSED

1 SMALL YELLOW ONION, DICED

1 GREEN BELL PEPPER, DICED

15oz CAN TOMATO SAUCE

2 TABLESPOONS KETCHUP

1 TABLESPOON WORCESTERSHIRE SAUCE

1/2 TEASPOON SALT

1/2 TEASPOON BLACK PEPPER

TO FREEZE AND COOK LATER

1. LABEL YOUR FREEZER BAG WITH THE NAME OF THE RECIPE, COOKING INSTRUCTIONS, AND "USE BY" DATE (THREE MONTHS FROM WHEN YOU PREPPED THE MEAL).
2. ADD ALL INGREDIENTS TO FREEZER BAG.
3. REMOVE AS MUCH AIR AS POSSIBLE FROM BAG, SEAL, & FREEZE.

TO COOK AND ENJOY

1. THAW FREEZER MEAL OVERNIGHT IN REFRIGERATOR, OR IN MORNING IN WATER.
2. ADD CONTENTS OF FREEZER BAG TO CROCKPOT.
3. COOK ON "LOW" SETTING FOR 4-6 HOURS IN A 6-QUART CROCKPOT.

NUTRITIONAL INFORMATION

SERVING SIZE: 3/4 CUP
FAT: 1g

SODIUM: 850mg
CARBS: 38g

SUGAR: 6g
PROTEIN: 13g

LENTIL VEGETABLE SOUP

SERVES 6

INGREDIENTS

15oz CAN DICED TOMATOES, UNDRAINED

4 CLOVES GARLIC, MINCED

1 TABLESPOON ITALIAN SEASONING

1 TEASPOON BLACK PEPPER

2 CUPS DRIED UNCOOKED LENTILS, RINSED

1 SMALL YELLOW ONION, DICED

2 OZ BABY SPINACH

2 RIBS CELERY, DICED

4 CARROTS, PEELED & DICED

8 CUPS LOW-SODIUM VEGETABLE BROTH (NOT NEEDED UNTIL DAY OF COOKING)

1 TEASPOON SALT

TO FREEZE AND COOK LATER

1. LABEL YOUR FREEZER BAG WITH THE NAME OF THE RECIPE, COOKING INSTRUCTIONS, AND "USE BY" DATE (THREE MONTHS FROM WHEN YOU PREPPED THE MEAL).
2. ADD ALL INGREDIENTS EXCEPT BROTH TO FREEZER BAG.
3. REMOVE AS MUCH AIR AS POSSIBLE FROM BAG, SEAL, & FREEZE.

TO COOK AND ENJOY

1. THAW FREEZER MEAL OVERNIGHT IN REFRIGERATOR, OR IN MORNING IN WATER.
2. ADD CONTENTS OF FREEZER BAG & BROTH TO CROCK-POT.
3. COOK ON "LOW" SETTING FOR 6-8 HOURS IN A 6-QUART CROCKPOT.

NUTRITIONAL INFORMATION

SERVING SIZE: 2 CUPS
FAT: 1g

SODIUM: 770mg
CARBS: 53g

SUGAR: 10g
PROTEIN: 18g

SPINACH ENCHILADAS

SERVES 5

INGREDIENTS

4oz COLBY JACK CHEESE, SHREDDED (NOT NEEDED UNTIL DAY OF COOKING)

1 TEASPOON ONION POWDER

1/2 TEASPOON GARLIC POWDER

10oz FRESH BABY SPINACH

15oz CAN TOMATO SAUCE

1/2 TEASPOON CRUSHED RED PEPPER FLAKES

1.5 TEASPOONS CHILI POWDER

TEN 6" ROUND FLOUR TORTILLAS (NOT NEEDED UNTIL DAY OF COOKING)

1/2 TEASPOON GROUND CUMIN

1/2 TEASPOON SALT

TO FREEZE AND COOK LATER

1. LABEL YOUR FREEZER BAG WITH THE NAME OF THE RECIPE, COOKING INSTRUCTIONS, AND "USE BY" DATE (THREE MONTHS FROM WHEN YOU PREPPED THE MEAL).
2. ADD ALL INGREDIENTS, EXCEPT CHEESE & TORTILLAS, TO FREEZER BAG.
3. REMOVE AS MUCH AIR AS POSSIBLE FROM BAG, SEAL, & FREEZE.

TO COOK AND ENJOY

1. THAW FREEZER MEAL OVERNIGHT IN REFRIGERATOR, OR IN MORNING IN WATER.
2. ADD CONTENTS OF FREEZER BAG TO CROCKPOT.
3. COOK ON "LOW" SETTING FOR 4-6 HOURS IN A 6-QUART CROCKPOT.
4. STIR IN 1/4 CUP SHREDDED CHEESE. REMOVE MIXTURE FROM CROCKPOT AND USE TO FILL TORTILLAS. PLACE BACK IN SLOW COOKER, SEAM-SIDE DOWN.
5. COVER W/ REMAINING CHEESE & COOK FOR AN ADDITIONAL 10 MINUTES, OR UNTIL CHEESE IS MELTED.

NUTRITIONAL INFORMATION

SERVING SIZE: 2 ENCHILADAS
FAT: 10g

SODIUM: 1190mg
CARBS: 34g

SUGAR: 3g
PROTEIN: 11g

EASY REFRIED BEANS

SERVES 8

INGREDIENTS

4-15oz CANS PINTO BEANS, UNDRAINED

1 SMALL YELLOW ONION, DICED

4 CLOVES GARLIC, MINCED

THE JUICE OF ONE LIME

1 TEASPOON CHILI POWDER

1 TEASPOON GROUND CUMIN

TO FREEZE AND COOK LATER

1. LABEL YOUR FREEZER BAG WITH THE NAME OF THE RECIPE, COOKING INSTRUCTIONS, AND "USE BY" DATE (THREE MONTHS FROM WHEN YOU PREPPED THE MEAL).
2. ADD ALL INGREDIENTS TO FREEZER BAG.
3. REMOVE AS MUCH AIR AS POSSIBLE FROM BAG, SEAL, & FREEZE.

TO COOK AND ENJOY

1. THAW FREEZER MEAL OVERNIGHT IN REFRIGERATOR, OR IN MORNING IN WATER.
2. ADD CONTENTS OF FREEZER BAG TO CROCKPOT.
3. COOK ON "LOW" SETTING FOR 6-8 HOURS IN A 6-QUART CROCKPOT.
4. PUREE TO DESIRED CONSISTENCY W/ IMMERSION BLENDER OR REGULAR COUNTERTOP BLENDER.

NUTRITIONAL INFORMATION

SERVING SIZE: 2/3 CUP
FAT: 0g
SODIUM: 790mg
CARBS: 34g
SUGAR: 1g
PROTEIN: 11g

TOMATO BASIL SOUP

SERVES 9

INGREDIENTS

4 TABLESPOONS UNSALTED BUTTER

15-20 BASIL LEAVES

28oz CAN WHOLE PEELED TOMATOES, UNDRAINED

15oz CAN TOMATO SAUCE

16oz VEGETABLE BROTH

16oz HEAVY WHIPPING CREAM (NOT NEEDED UNTIL DAY OF COOKING)

1/2 TEASPOON BLACK PEPPER

1/2 TEASPOON SALT

TO FREEZE AND COOK LATER

1. LABEL YOUR FREEZER BAG WITH THE NAME OF THE RECIPE, COOKING INSTRUCTIONS, AND "USE BY" DATE (THREE MONTHS FROM WHEN YOU PREPPED THE MEAL).
2. ADD ALL INGREDIENTS, EXCEPT CREAM, TO FREEZER BAG.
3. REMOVE AS MUCH AIR AS POSSIBLE FROM BAG, SEAL, & FREEZE.

TO COOK AND ENJOY

1. THAW FREEZER MEAL OVERNIGHT IN REFRIGERATOR, OR IN MORNING IN WATER.
2. ADD CONTENTS OF FREEZER BAG TO CROCKPOT.
3. COOK ON "LOW" SETTING FOR 4-6 HOURS IN A 6-QUART CROCKPOT.
4. ADD HEAVY WHIPPING CREAM & STIR TO COMBINE.
5. PUREE TO DESIRED CONSISTENCY W/ IMMERSION BLENDER OR REGULAR COUNTERTOP BLENDER.

NUTRITIONAL INFORMATION

SERVING SIZE: 1 CUP
FAT: 24g
SODIUM: 700mg
CARBS: 10g
SUGAR: 4g
PROTEIN: 2g

BLACK BEAN SOUP

SERVES 6

INGREDIENTS

1 SMALL YELLOW ONION, DICED

2 RIBS CELERY, CHOPPED

4 CLOVES GARLIC, MINCED

2 CUPS VEGETABLE BROTH

4-15oz CANS BLACK BEANS, DRAINED & RINSED

15oz CAN DICED TOMATOES, UNDRAINED

1 LARGE CARROT, PEELED & DICED

1 TABLESPOON CHILI POWDER

2 TEASPOONS GROUND CUMIN

1/2 TEASPOON BLACK PEPPER

1/2 TEASPOON SALT

TO FREEZE AND COOK LATER

1. LABEL YOUR FREEZER BAG WITH THE NAME OF THE RECIPE, COOKING INSTRUCTIONS, AND "USE BY" DATE (THREE MONTHS FROM WHEN YOU PREPPED THE MEAL).
2. ADD ALL INGREDIENTS TO FREEZER BAG.
3. REMOVE AS MUCH AIR AS POSSIBLE FROM BAG, SEAL, & FREEZE.

TO COOK AND ENJOY

1. THAW FREEZER MEAL OVERNIGHT IN REFRIGERATOR, OR IN MORNING IN WATER.
2. ADD CONTENTS OF FREEZER BAG TO CROCKPOT.
3. COOK ON "LOW" SETTING FOR 6-8 HOURS IN A 6-QUART CROCKPOT.
4. PUREE TO DESIRED CONSISTENCY W/ IMMERSION BLENDER OR REGULAR COUNTERTOP BLENDER.

NUTRITIONAL INFORMATION

SERVING SIZE: 1 1/2 CUPS
FAT: 0g

SODIUM: 1010mg
CARBS: 53g

SUGAR: 9g
PROTEIN: 21g

VEGAN KORMA

SERVES 6

INGREDIENTS

15oz CAN UNSWEETENED COCONUT MILK

1" FRESH GINGER ROOT, GRATED

6 CLOVES GARLIC, MINCED

1 CUP FROZEN PEAS

2 MEDIUM SWEET POTATOES, PEELED & CHOPPED

2 CARROTS, PEELED & CHOPPED

8oz FROZEN CAULIFLOWER FLORETS

1 SMALL YELLOW ONION, DICED

1 JALEPENO PEPPER, DESEEDED & DICED

1 TABLESPOON GARAM MASALA

1 TEASPOON CURRY POWDER

1/2 TEASPOON SALT

TO FREEZE AND COOK LATER

1. LABEL YOUR FREEZER BAG WITH THE NAME OF THE RECIPE, COOKING INSTRUCTIONS, AND "USE BY" DATE (THREE MONTHS FROM WHEN YOU PREPPED THE MEAL).
2. ADD ALL INGREDIENTS TO FREEZER BAG.
3. REMOVE AS MUCH AIR AS POSSIBLE FROM BAG, SEAL, & FREEZER.

TO COOK AND ENJOY

1. THAW FREEZER MEAL OVERNIGHT IN REFRIGERATOR, OR IN MORNING IN WATER.
2. ADD CONTENTS OF FREEZER BAG TO CROCKPOT.
3. COOK ON "LOW" SETTING FOR 6-8 HOURS IN A 6-QUART CROCKPOT.

NUTRITIONAL INFORMATION

SERVING SIZE: 1 CUP
FAT: 11g

SODIUM: 270mg
CARBS: 20g

SUGAR: 6g
PROTEIN: 3g

VEGETABLE MINESTRONE SOUP

SERVES 6

INGREDIENTS

15oz CAN KIDNEY BEANS, DRAINED & RINSED

15oz CAN CANNELLINI BEANS, DRAINED & RINSED

28oz CAN DICED TOMATOES, UNDRAINED

2 TABLESPOONS ITALIAN SEASONING

4 LARGE CARROTS, PEELED & DICED

3 CUPS GREEN BEANS, ENDS CUT OFF & CHOPPED

2oz FRESH BABY SPINACH

1 SMALL YELLOW ONION, DICED

4 CLOVES GARLIC, MINCED

6 CUPS LOW-SODIUM VEGETABLE BROTH (NOT NEEDED UNTIL DAY OF COOKING)

1 CUP UNCOOKED ELBOW MACARONI (NOT NEEDED UNTIL DAY OF COOKING)

1/2 TEASPOON BLACK PEPPER

1 TEASPOON HONEY

1 BAY LEAF

TO FREEZE AND COOK LATER

1. LABEL YOUR FREEZER BAG WITH THE NAME OF THE RECIPE, COOKING INSTRUCTIONS, AND "USE BY" DATE (THREE MONTHS FROM WHEN YOU PREPPED THE MEAL).
2. ADD ALL INGREDIENTS, EXCEPT BROTH & MACARONI, TO FREEZER BAG.
3. REMOVE AS MUCH AIR AS POSSIBLE FROM BAG, SEAL, & FREEZE.

TO COOK AND ENJOY

1. THAW FREEZER MEAL OVERNIGHT IN REFRIGERATOR, OR IN MORNING IN WATER.
2. ADD CONTENTS OF FREEZER BAG & BROTH TO CROCK-POT.
3. COOK ON "LOW" SETTING FOR 6-8 HOURS IN A 6-QUART CROCKPOT.
4. ADD MACARONI & COOK FOR AN ADDITIONAL 30 MINUTES.
5. REMOVE BAY LEAF & SERVE.

NUTRITIONAL INFORMATION

SERVING SIZE: 2 CUPS
FAT: 0g
SODIUM: 1390mg
CARBS: 60g
SUGAR: 13g
PROTEIN: 12g

Seasoning PACKETS

HOMEMADE AU JUS SEASONING PACKET

2 TEASPOONS BEEF BOUILLON GRANULES

1 TEASPOON SOY SAUCE

1/4 TEASPOON GARLIC POWDER

1/4 TEASPOON PEPPER

HOMEMADE RANCH SEASONING PACKET

1 TABLESPOON PARSLEY

1 TEASPOON GARLIC POWDER

1 TEASPOON ONION POWDER

1 TEASPOON DRIED MINCED ONION FLAKES

3/4 TEASPOON DILL

1/2 TEASPOON PEPPER

1/2 TEASPOON SALT

HOMEMADE TACO SEASONING PACKET

1 TABLESPOON CHILI POWDER

1 TEASPOON PEPPER

1/2 TEASPOON OF THE FOLLOWING:

- SALT
- CUMIN
- RED PEPPER FLAKES
- PAPRIKA
- OREGANO
- GARLIC POWDER
- ONION POWDER

HAPPY FREEZING!

Freezer cooking has been a part of my life for over nine years now and I don't think I'll ever go back to scrambling for dinner every night at 5 p.m. Making slow cooker freezer meals has become a way of life and my favorite shortcut to saving time and money while still eating healthy.

I never imagined writing freezer recipes would become a full-time job for me, but I love it. Every day, people send me emails and messages on social media telling me how my recipes changed their lives. I am so thankful for their encouragement, and I would love to hear about your adventures in freezer cooking, too.

Please send me an email or reach out on Facebook, Instagram, or Pinterest.

Until then,

Kelly

CPSIA information can be obtained
at www.ICGtesting.com
Printed in the USA
BVHW052159011218
532560BV00008B/2/P

9 781944 134136